Sacrifice
of
Praise

Sacrifice
of
Praise

Myra Noel Johnson

Prairie Light
— MEDIA —

Published in the United States of America

Cover photo by kevron2001 from Getty Images, licensed for use via Canva Pro

Cover design by Myra Johnson

All Scripture verses taken from the King James Bible.

ISBN 978-1-965204-01-6

Prairie Light Media
PO Box 9073
Fargo, ND 58106
www.prairielightmedia.org

Dedication

To my husband, Rob.
Without you, I would never have finished this book.

To my mom, Dollie Noel.
Your fervent prayers and faithfulness encourage and challenge
me to be more like you and more like Christ.

In memory of my dad, Stephen Noel.
His lessons and wisdom still help guide me.

Contents

Preface

God gave me the title and burden for this book in 2013, when my journey of miscarriages and secondary infertility began. I started writing then, but God had eleven more years of work to do on me before I was ready to finish it. I had more lessons to learn and more valleys to travel.

Just when I decided I wasn't up to the task of writing a book, I mentioned it in a conversation with my husband, telling him I didn't think I could do it. He immediately encouraged me to write it. Then he told people I was writing a book! With that nudge, I started working on it again. I am thankful God used Rob's excitement and encouragement to keep me from quitting.

Travel, ministry, more miscarriages, and poor health interrupted me often. Brain fog from chronic illness kept me from focusing on it for months at a time. Slowly, God gave me one article or devotion at a time. When I listened to messages or studied the Bible during my devotions, I jotted down verses and thoughts that I felt should be in the book. I filled notebooks with notes, waiting for days of clear thinking so I could write. Slowly, this book took shape.

At every turn, I prayed God would lead me and use me to bring Him glory and to help others. Obedience to God, bringing Him glory, and helping others are my only reasons for writing this book. I pray God encourages you or equips you to encourage others through my failings and my testimony of God's greatness and faithfulness.

Valleys

Have you ever walked through a valley so dark you secretly feared you might never see the light of day again? Are you in a valley so endless and deep, you think you'll never climb out of it?

Some valleys are short and intense, shaking us, but ending quickly as we see God work on our behalf. Other valleys seem to go on forever, often with no hope in sight of leaving it. Our weakness cries that we cannot stand any more. Satan whispers God has forgotten us and we are unloved; better just to give up now. Other valleys we know will only end when we stand in the presence of our Saviour.

I have been through some of these long valleys. They seem never-ending and you feel alone, broken, abandoned, even crushed. However, if you listen closely, you will hear a voice so low and tender that sometimes you do not hear it clearly in the busyness of life, only in the lonely valleys. It is such a sweet, and dear voice, that any valley is worth enduring just to hear it better.

Your valley is not the same as mine. Some valleys are physical pain. Others are the valley of death, where our loved ones leave us—or we are the ones saying goodbye. Some are valleys of betrayal, abuse, or other loss. Sometimes a combination of trials makes our valley dark. Your valley may be one I could not even imagine.

For a Christian, they all have one thing in common. The Lily of the valleys is there. We are never alone, regardless of how alone we feel. He loves, leads, teaches, rebukes, refines, and/or grows us, so we may bring Him more glory and be more like Him.

God put this book on my heart as He led me through a series of valleys, each darker than the last. Lyme Disease, long undiagnosed, had brought me to a place of constant pain and growing weakness. I didn't know what was wrong, so I continued to push through the pain, falling further behind in work, ministry, and personal life. Then I married a wonderful man, and we began deputation to go to Botswana, Africa. I was 42 when we married, so we knew having children was possible, but not guaranteed. Over the next 3 years, six pregnancies ended in early miscarriage. Each miscarriage weakened my immune system, allowing the Lyme Disease and co-infections to take over. Grief, illness, inflammation, brain fog, weakness, and wrong focus brought a depression I never shared and tried to hide. I put a smile on my face, walked into each new church, talked about Botswana and wished I could go home and crawl into bed so the pain, dizziness, and weakness could temporarily disappear in sleep. Not every meeting was this hard, but many were. I often held myself up by holding onto a pew, table, or wall. At one point, I was growing so weak and the pain was so intense, I honestly didn't expect to live to see Africa. I began praying if God took me Home, that He would give my husband another wife so he would have help in Africa.

Instead of taking me Home, God led me to people who could help me physically, gave moments of clarity through the brain fog, and began working on my spirit. More valleys followed, but the lessons I learned helped me walk the new valleys with peace instead of turmoil.

The following devotions are some God graciously gave me during my own valleys. Sometimes He gently rebuked me for my reactions and focus. Often, He comforted me in my pain. At other times, God strengthened me for the task ahead. But in all of them, He led and taught me. God's lessons and encouragements brought me through my darkest valleys and changed me. I wanted to share them with you. Even now, His words still comfort and encourage me.

I would never have chosen the valleys I walked through, but I am forever thankful that God led me through them. God used them to change me, and that change was worth all the pain.

We all encounter valleys in our lives. My prayer is that these devotions will serve as a source of encouragement, strength, and help for you, just as they did for me in my own valleys. Join me on my journey from despair to joy and discover the hope and comfort that only comes from the Lily of the valleys.

Because all I am is His,
Myra

Chapter One

Do You Know the Lily of the Valley?

I cannot jump into the following chapters without saying a few words about having a genuine relationship with God. If you don't know Him personally, you may glean some knowledge or help from the chapters that follow, but they will not be as powerful in your life. Because all of them are based on knowing the God of Heaven as your very own Father.

When I was a young child, I heard a message that woke me to the fact that we are all sinners. This was a surprise to me. I thought I was a pretty good little girl. I learned that not only are we sinners, but God hates sin and cannot let sin into heaven. The result of sin is death, and that death is separation from God. For those who reject Him, the end is eternity in hell. This realization disturbed me. I didn't like anyone being unhappy with me, and I hated pain. The reality that God wasn't pleased with me and I was going to hell shook me.

When I asked my parents about it, they shared the truth with me, but all I caught was that I was in trouble and I needed to pray. That day, I followed everything they said, but I didn't trust God. I trusted my prayer. I was 'doing' everything necessary to make sure God accepted me and I didn't go to hell. They thought I understood the truth because I agreed with them, and said what I thought everyone wanted to hear.

For years, I tried to be good. I was often pretty good at faking it and reading people to please them (except with my siblings). I even won the annual Christian Character Award for our Christian school when I was 11 years old. No one knew I was struggling with doubt. Every time the doubts arose, I pushed them down by reminding myself that I had prayed. That meant God had to save me.

When I was 11, I remember our pastor preaching on the following passage.

> 1 Thessalonians 4:13-18 "But I would not have you to
> be ignorant, brethren, concerning them which are
> asleep, that ye sorrow not, even as others which have
> no hope. [14]For if we believe that Jesus died and rose
> again, even so them also which sleep in Jesus will God
> bring with him. [15]For this we say unto you by the word
> of the Lord, that we which are alive *and* remain unto
> the coming of the Lord shall not prevent them which
> are asleep. [16]For the Lord himself shall descend from
> heaven with a shout, with the voice of the archangel,
> and with the trump of God: and the dead in Christ shall
> rise first: [17]Then we which are alive *and* remain shall
> be caught up together with them in the clouds, to meet
> the Lord in the air: and so shall we ever be with the
> Lord. [18]Wherefore comfort one another with these words."

These verses teach about the rapture: when Christ raises the dead saints and takes all living Christians to heaven. The last verse says, "Wherefore comfort one another with these words." I knew I had a problem because the words in this passage didn't comfort me. They terrified me. I had no blessed hope.[1] As he preached about the rapture and end-time events, I grew more uncomfortable. I started sleeping on my side, afraid that if I was lying on my back, I would see Him come in the air, but leave me behind. A child's mind works in funny ways, but there was nothing funny about my fear and God's conviction.

That summer we went to family camp. One night during the message, God showed me what was missing. I realized that I had prayed, tried to be good, and fooled many people, but I had never trusted the work Jesus did on the cross for my salvation. Instead of trusting, I was still trying to gain God's favor, and it was impossible. I was still lost. That night, I turned from my futile efforts to appease or please God and trusted Christ as my Savior. This is the repentance Paul preached to both Jews and Gentiles.

> Acts 20:21 "Testifying both to the Jews, and also to the Greeks, repentance toward God, and faith toward our Lord Jesus Christ."

I want to share some verses with you that helped me, and I encourage you to examine yourself to make sure you are a child of God.

First, we must realize we need a Saviour. The Bible is full of verses that show us our sinful condition. Romans 3:23 puts it succinctly:

> Romans 3:23 "For all have sinned, and come short of the glory of God;"

This doesn't leave any room for "I'm a good person." Every single person has sinned. Romans 6:23 tells us the penalty of being a sinner.

> Romans 6:23a "For the wages of sin *is* death…"

Many ask how God can condemn sinners to hell, but truthfully, we earn it. Our sin separates us from God, according to

---

[1] Titus 2:13 "Looking for that blessed hope, and the glorious appearing of the great God and our Saviour Jesus Christ;"

Isaiah 59:2. Jesus told Nicodemus that those who didn't believe in Him are *already* condemned.

> John 3:17-18 "For God sent not his Son into the world to condemn the world; but that the world through him might be saved. [18]He that believeth on him is not condemned: but he that believeth not is condemned already, because he hath not believed in the name of the only begotten Son of God."

If you doubt you are a sinner deserving death, look at the law in Exodus 20. If we have ever taken God's name in vain (using it lightly or as an exclamation or curse word), failed to honor our parents completely, lusted after someone, stolen even the smallest thing, or any other host of "little sins", we are guilty of death. James 2:10 tells us that if we have offended in one point, we are guilty of the whole law. We are in trouble.

If we stopped here, we would all be without hope. But God, in His great mercy, made a way for us to be reconciled to Him. God's holiness, justice, and judgment makes His mercy, grace, and love so much more amazing. The last half of Romans 6:23 gives us hope.

> Romans 6:23 "For the wages of sin *is* death; but the gift of God *is* eternal life through Jesus Christ our Lord."

God, knowing we could not save ourselves, provided a Redeemer. Jesus Christ, God in the flesh, came to die in our place. He took the death penalty for us.

> John 3:16 "For God so loved the world, that he gave his only begotten Son, that whosoever believeth in him should not perish, but have everlasting life."

There is nothing we can do to earn God's favor or a place in Heaven with Him. Our only hope is trusting in Jesus. This was where I messed up as a child. I believed I was a sinner, and that Jesus had died for my sins, but I didn't trust Him. I trusted my prayer. If I prayed certain words, God must save me. That was a work, not faith.

Titus 3:5 "Not by works of righteousness which we have done, but according to his mercy he saved us, by the washing of regeneration, and renewing of the Holy Ghost;"

When I realized I was lost, I quit trying to appease God and do all the right things and cast myself on His mercy, trusting the work Jesus did on the cross. If you are not sure you know God, please talk to someone. If you don't have anyone you can talk to, please reach out to me. My greatest joy is pointing others to Jesus Christ and helping them have a real, vibrant relationship with Him.

Chapter Two

Sacrifice of Praise

Hebrews 13:12-15 "Wherefore Jesus also, that he might sanctify the people with his own blood, suffered without the gate. [13]Let us go forth therefore unto him without the camp, bearing his reproach. [14]For here have we no continuing city, but we seek one to come. [15]By him therefore let us offer the sacrifice of praise to God continually, that is, the fruit of *our* lips giving thanks to his name."

We rarely think of sacrifice and praise in the same sentence. We typically think of praise in terms of joy when it comes pouring out of an abundant and overflowing heart. But think about it. Sometimes praise is a sacrifice. It is easier to cry, sleep, complain, or give up when our hearts break, our bodies are exhausted, the enemy attacks, or life is overwhelming.

During these times, we must *choose* to praise God. We make this choice because it is right, because He commands it, and because He is holy and worthy of it, not because it is easy. Choose to sing through the heartache, discouragement, fatigue, or pain. We must offer our praise to God as a sacrifice that is well-pleasing to Him, not because we feel like it, but because He is worthy.

God commands us to praise. In the Old Testament, when God assigned the Levites their work in the service of God, He gave some the specific task of singing and praising God.

> 1 Chronicles 23:5 "Moreover four thousand were porters; and four thousand praised the LORD with the instruments which I made, said David, to praise therewith."

In 1 Samuel 29-30, we learn David faced a time when praise did not come naturally. He was living in the land of the Philistines because Saul tried to kill him many times. When the Philistines went to battle against Israel, they refused to let David and his men fight for fear they would turn on them in the battle. The Philistine kings sent them back to Ziklag.

David and his men traveled three days to get home. When they arrived, they found the city burned and all their women and children were gone. This horror would have been bad enough, but after they wept until they had no more power to weep, David faced another trial: the threat of death. The men started talking about stoning David. These men lived, camped, hid, suffered, and fought with David. Now they blamed him for their loss. Somehow, it was his fault that the enemy burned their city and took their families captive.

It would have been so easy (and, in many people's opinion, acceptable) to throw up his hands and complain about his circumstances, lash out in anger, or sink into despair. Today, many would expect him to post it on social media, not only about the loss of his family and home, but also those lousy friends and fellow-soldiers who turned on him. Instead, we read this intriguing statement, "…but David encouraged himself in the LORD his God."

He strengthened himself in his God. Having read the Psalms of David and the account of his life from Scripture, I can only think of one way David accomplished this; by reminding himself of God's faithfulness and power in the past and God's promises for the future.

God had never failed David, and He wouldn't do so now. Besides, God had promised David that he would be king. There was no way God would let them kill David today because God always keeps His promises. Having encouraged himself, He turned to God and asked for help and direction in his current dilemma.

While we don't have an account of David praising God until after the battle, looking at David's life, I believe he did. To recount God's past glories and how He has proved faithful is to offer praise for what He has done and who He is.

God tells us to give thanks in all things. That includes giving thanks during the bad times, too. We can give thanks and praise to God, even in the valley. Not because of our circumstances, but because of who God is.

David's confidence was not in his ability or power, but in the power, unchangeable character, and promises of God. Our confidence, peace, and joy are not in our situation or our ability to change it, but in the character of an unchangeable and holy God. The valley is a good place to remind ourselves of some things the Bible says about God and His character:

He cannot lie. (Titus 1:2)

He is all-powerful. (Matthew 28:18)

He loves us without end. (Jeremiah 31:3)

He promises never to leave or forsake us. (Hebrews 13:5)

He intercedes for us. (Romans 8:27)

He promises to work all things for good. (Romans 8:28)

He is the only wise God. (1 Timothy 1:17)

He is our Redeemer. (Psalm 78:35)

He is compassionate and merciful. (Lamentations 2:11)

This is just a small sample. There is so much more to learn about Him. Understanding who God is, we can offer the sacrifices of thanksgiving and praise, even in life's darkest valley. We can still praise and thank Him when our heart is breaking, our health is gone, our circumstances seem impossible, and we feel like praising least.

Psalm 18:3 "I will call upon the LORD, *who is worthy* to be praised: so shall I be saved from mine enemies."

What keeps you from praising God? What does Satan offer you as an excuse to not praise and give thanks? Reject Satan's lies and look at what God says about praise.

Psalm 22:3 "But thou *art* holy, *O thou* that inhabitest the praises of Israel."

Psalm 50:23 "Whoso offereth praise glorifieth me: and to him that ordereth *his* conversation *aright* will I shew the salvation of God."

Psalm 33:1-2 "Rejoice in the LORD, O ye righteous: *for* praise is comely for the upright. ²Praise the LORD with harp: sing unto him with the psaltery *and* an instrument of ten strings."

This is a daily walk, not a onetime lesson. If our focus shifts, our peace will flee. If we keep our eyes on Him and praise, there is peace amid the biggest storm or string of storms. I have proved this.

During the hardest season of my life, God challenged me to praise Him, anyway. Chronic illness, incessant pain, and losing my children in miscarriages brought me to the place where I felt like I had nothing left to give. Although I continued to go through the motions of life and ministry, my heart wasn't in it.

I didn't want to praise, but I saw the command and (reluctantly) listened to the Holy Spirit. My focus had been so inward, I didn't know where to start. So, I began singing songs of praise. I didn't feel joyful, but I praised anyway. When I couldn't sing because of the tears, I played songs of praise. Then I searched for things to praise God for. Finally, I could praise Him for the valley, even though I didn't like it and didn't know why He was leading me through it. I chose to trust Him and praise Him for it *before* I saw the reason. This is when I really saw this concept of the sacrifice of praise and its blessings. When I practiced it, I found victory, peace, and even joy in my sorrow. When I focused on my pain, peace fled.

Isaiah 26:3 Thou wilt keep *him* in perfect peace, *whose* mind *is* stayed *on thee:* because he trusteth in thee.

This verse gives us the key to peace: keep our minds focused on God and trust Him. What valley are you facing today? Do you feel as if you won't make it through? Let me encourage you to offer our deserving God the sacrifice of praise. Start with music. If you can't sing yet, listen to music that praises God. Follow this with praise for His goodness and answered prayer in the past. Finally, in faith, praise Him for the valley you walk today, trusting that He will keep His promise and work it for good. Watch Him replace despair with grace and peace as you offer Him a sacrifice of praise.

Chapter Three

All Things

Romans 8:28 "And we know that all things work together for good to them that love God, to them who are the called according to his purpose."

I sat with my Bible in my lap as tears streamed down my face. The past few months had been the hardest of my young life. Disappointment, disillusionment, guilt, and heartbreak vied for first place. I had prayed and sought counsel, but no peace came. I didn't understand why this trial had happened, although I knew my choices had contributed to it. No matter how much I tried, I couldn't learn, heal, and move on. I prayed, cried, and looked for answers. Here I was, pestering God about it again.

This time, He brought me back to this passage. I reread it, and told God, "But I brought some of this on myself. How can I expect you to work it for good when I was foolish?"

He replied, "All things."

"What about their part in bringing this hurt?"

"All things."

"What if this kind of hurt happens again? How can I trust anyone else?"

"All things."

God answered every question I had that day with the same words. "All things."

It is easy to see God's hand in certain trials. We expect Him to show His hand mighty and we anticipate deliverance. In other trials, we struggle to keep that focus and hope. How can this be good? Can I really expect God to sort out this mess and bring good from it? It may seem to be an impossible situation, with no end in sight. How can a bitter betrayal or abuse work for good? We may struggle to believe God will keep this promise if we are responsible (even in part) for our own trouble. The simplicity of this verse is breathtaking.

And we know...

This part speaks with certainty. There is no room for wishy-washy hoping. This verse leaves no wiggle room for doubt. We know this to be a fact. If it wasn't, God would not have it in His Word. We may not see how He can possibly do it, but we can trust Him. After all, Titus 1:2 tells us He is "God, that cannot lie."

All things...

All. Not some or most, all. Every single trial that comes into our lives falls under this promise. Does this include trouble caused by someone else's sin? Yes. Is hardship that comes because of my sin or foolishness covered? Yes. What about "random" trials like health or financial crisis? Yes, they're covered too. Can this possibly apply to loneliness and overwhelming grief that comes from the death of one we love most? Yes, this promise covers even that. Are you in the middle of a trial that has gone on for months or years? You guessed it. It's covered. Minor disappointments that we almost feel guilty for being

upset over? Yes, those too. It even covers the trial where someone is actively trying to destroy our lives. Nothing is too big or
too small to fit this promise.

Work together for good...

Do you notice what God does not say here? We do not find
any qualifiers. It doesn't say, "may work together for good".
This is a promise that you can count on. Even when you cannot
see how God can work it for good, trust Him to keep His Word.
Remember, He is Truth. He will work it together for good. At the
time, I did not see how God could work this trial for good, but
looking back, I see how much He taught me and how He used it
in my life. I see His protection and how His plan was so much
better than mine, and I am completely thankful for going
through that trial now.

He also does not say "all things *are* good." This sometimes
trips us up. We wonder, "How can this possibly be good?" He
didn't say it was good. He said it works together for good. There
are many terrible things throughout history that God worked for
good. It was despicable for Joseph's brothers to sell him into
slavery, but God worked it for good.

It was a nightmare for Esther to be taken forcibly to the
king's house of women, never to return home, but God worked
it for good. Remember, she was in the house of women for at
least a year, uncertain when she would be called to go in to the
heathen king. She had no reason to believe he would choose her
to be queen, and she probably had no desire to be the queen of a
heathen nation. All she knew was the king's men stole her, his
servants kept her for the pleasure of a Gentile king, and she
would never see home again. If the keeper of women never sent
her to the king, she would remain in the house of virgins. If they
sent her to the king, but he didn't choose her to be queen, she
would go to the house of the concubines. What a horrible
prospect! Yet God worked it together for good, putting her in a
position to be used to save God's people.

To them that love God, to them who are the called according to his purpose...

I wonder if this is sometimes the part that catches us most. We tell ourselves, or the enemy whispers, "This is your fault. You didn't love God enough, or you didn't have enough faith." As if a loving God will protect us from all hardship. Don't believe that lie. Look at great and godly people in Scripture and history who loved God and suffered greatly. God loves us enough to put us through the fire that will refine us.

Possibly, the trial that has come into our life is to teach us to love Him more. Maybe we love ourselves a little (or a lot) more than we love Him. When I was going through this, I loved God, but honestly, I wanted my way, too. Going through the trials in my life has refined and increased my love for God. A good place to start is to ask, "Lord, do I truly love You? If my love is lacking, show me and teach me to love You more." When we have the focus of our love right, we can move on to trust this promise.

This lesson came back to me years later. Poor health and multiple miscarriages left me broken and teetering on the edge of bitterness. I had lost my focus. Once again, God brought me back to this verse. Again, I argued. How could this possibly be for good? His reply was the same as it had been 15 years earlier. Focusing on this promise, and choosing to believe it, restored the peace I was missing. Although I didn't yet see the good He promised, I trusted Him. That was enough.

Looking back now, I can see some of what God was doing. I see His work in my heart, refining me, making me more like Him. I can also see how He has used this to allow me to help other ladies who are hurting. If I had not endured the pain, I would never have understood, or even cared, as much. To be honest, I was self-righteous and short on mercy and grace when I was young. God couldn't use me the way He wanted until He put me through the fire. I couldn't understand when I was in the middle of it, but hindsight allows me to see how He used "all things" for good. If you don't understand how this trial can be for the good, trust Him. He promised, and He always keeps His promises.

Learning to rest in this promise helped me walk later valleys with peace. I didn't have to understand. I just had to take Him at His Word and rest in His promise.

"The storms are guided by the hands
which were nailed to the cross."
-John Newton

Chapter Four

Rejoice Alway

Philippians 4:4 "Rejoice in the Lord alway: and again I say, Rejoice."

God reminded me of this while my husband and I were on deputation to go to Africa. After three miscarriages and disintegrating health, I had found some help. I was slowly (but not steadily) regaining some health and relief from the constant pain. We were in a mission apartment. It was a lovely apartment, decorated nicely with verses on the walls. Above the desk, hung the quote, "Rejoice in the LORD alway..." at eye level. I loved it. It was a constant reminder always to rejoice, not just when things were going my way. This command means I am to always "be full of cheer and calmly happy" according to Strong's Concordance.

The day before I noticed this plaque, I was full of cheer and calmly happy. It was such an easy day to rejoice. I woke with plenty of energy (rare for me), accomplished all the tasks I set for myself (very rare indeed), and the day went smoothly. It was an all-around good day, and those don't happen very often when you battle chronic illness. So, my heart was light, and it was effortless to rejoice.

The following day, I woke up hurting, more tired than the day before (although not nearly as tired as usual), and I didn't feel great. Feeling worse than the day before disappointed me. I had hoped yesterday was the beginning of a trend, not just one good day. Sitting on the couch with a cup of coffee, I looked over at that wall and saw the words, "Rejoice in the LORD alway…". I had to smile at the reminder. Maybe I need to put those words on my wall wherever I am.

After a couple of cups of coffee, a hot shower, and breakfast, I felt better. I was still tired, but better. I looked back over the past months and how rough they had been and realized it was a great day compared to the pain and poor health I had before. But more than that, God reminded me that regardless of how I feel, my circumstances, or what life brings, Christ commands me to rejoice.

Since that day, I have had many good days and many rough days. Shortly after this, another miscarriage wiped out all the progress I had made. Pain and fatigue returned with a vengeance. Some days were worse than others. In every one, I could find something to rejoice in when I looked for it. That is always the key: I have to look for it—it is my choice. I can look at the pain, disappointment, difficulties, or sorrow, or I can look at God and choose to rejoice in Him and praise Him.

I love 2 Chronicles 14. Asa, king of Judah, has had 10 years of peaceful reign. He wisely used this time to cleanse the land of the high places and idols and challenge Judah to seek the Lord. After 10 peaceful years, Zerah, the Ethiopian, brought 1,000,000 men to battle against Asa's army of 580,000. It was not a well-matched battle, but Asa and his men went out and set the battle in array. Asa did not ask God why He let this trouble come after his faithfulness. He prayed for help, but he began his pre-battle prayer with praise.

2 Chronicles 14:11 "And Asa cried unto the LORD his God, and said, LORD, it is nothing with thee to help, whether with many, or with them that have no power: help us, O LORD our God; for we rest on thee, and in thy name we go against this multitude. O LORD, thou art our God; let not man prevail against thee."

He did not wait until after the victory to praise God's might and power. He focused on it, drawing strength from remembering how powerful his God was before asking God for help.

God commands us to thank and praise Him.

Ephesians 5:18-20 "And be not drunk with wine, wherein is excess; but be filled with the Spirit; [19]Speaking to yourselves in psalms and hymns and spiritual songs, singing and making melody in your heart to the Lord; [20]Giving thanks always for all things unto God and the Father in the name of our Lord Jesus Christ;"

These verses are not a mere suggestion, but a command. The contrast in verse 18 shows us we need to be filled with the Spirit, controlled by Him, like someone controlled by the wine they have drunk. Have you ever seen an intoxicated person? They don't behave normally. The drink changes their behavior.

If we allow the Holy Spirit to control us by submitting to Him, we will behave differently. We will act like Christ. We will speak and sing godly songs, have a melody in our hearts, and give thanks always for all things.

I studied the command to rejoice in Philippians 4 and the surrounding circumstances. Paul was in prison when he wrote this. The Christians at Philippi were under severe persecution. Yet Paul instructed them to rejoice.

We find it easy to rejoice in good times, but we must remember to rejoice whether we're happy or sad, when we feel great or we're overwhelmed by pain, when life brings pleasant surprises or harsh disappointments. The command to rejoice applies whether others encourage, discourage, or betray us. Rejoice on the mountain, and in the valley, in the sunshine and in dark days. I can rejoice because I have a wonderful Saviour.

David wrote Psalm 34, looking back at the danger he faced with Abimelech. It is a psalm of praise born from a great trial.

> Psalm 34:1-3 "I will bless the LORD at all times: his praise *shall* continually *be* in my mouth. ²My soul shall make her boast in the LORD: the humble shall hear *thereof,* and be glad. ³O magnify the LORD with me, and let us exalt his name together."

The entire psalm focuses on God's great power, His help in trouble, and praising Him. I encourage you to read this psalm when you find yourself discouraged.

Sometimes we struggle to rejoice because our focus is on our trouble and pain instead of on God. Other times we struggle because we believe the lie that we cannot have joy while we hurt. Realizing joy and pain can live together helped me immensely, and I wrote the following post to celebrate that truth.

When Joy & Pain Live Together

Today would have been my due date for our last baby "born to Heaven." For the last few weeks, I've been contemplating what an adventure these first six months in Botswana would have been if we had been expecting, and preparing for, the arrival of this little one. (The guests we have with us this week would have had to schedule for another time.) But instead of holding, or preparing to hold, our child, we're celebrating his/her life in Heaven.

Our first baby would have been 2½ right now, or the second would have been 2, or… You get the picture. Images of what might have been have played through my mind. But in spite of the pain of loss, images of what *is* plays even stronger. You see, all six of our children are enjoying Heaven. All six of them see our Saviour's face. Not one of them will ever know the ache of loss, pain or bad health, the agony of betrayal, or the sadness of separation.

More glorious than that, they are enjoying Heaven and Jesus in the purest, most blessed way possible…without regret. No sorrow over sin or wrong decisions. No shame over having grieved God in this life. They get to enjoy the beauties of Jesus and Heaven in the purest innocence. No mother could ask for more than that for her children.

Yes, my arms are still empty. My heart still hurts. I still miss them every day, and more so on due dates and birthdays. Pregnancy announcements, birth announcements, and all the other milestones I see others celebrate still cause joy for them, mingled with sorrow for our loss. Yet in the midst of sadness, there is peace when I keep my mind stayed on Jesus. I will never hold them, or see them grow up here, but I will go to them one day. And for now, I can rejoice in remembering that Jesus gave them a great blessing when He gave them Heaven without the sorrow that comes from living on this fallen earth. And my mama's heart is content. Sad, but content. Because my God doeth all things well.

Sometimes we need help finding a reason to rejoice, so I would like to leave you with a few reasons that helped me turn from sorrowing to rejoicing.

We can rejoice because He has helped us in the past and will never leave us nor forsake us.

Psalm 63:7 "Because thou hast been my help, therefore in the shadow of thy wings will I rejoice."

Rejoice because He is holy and worthy of praise.

Psalm 97:12 "Rejoice in the LORD, ye righteous; and give thanks at the remembrance of his holiness."

Rejoice because He is faithful to keep His promises and powerful enough to do the impossible.

Psalm 68:4 "Sing unto God, sing praises to his name: extol him that rideth upon the heavens by his name JAH, and rejoice before him."

Rejoice because He commands it.

Psalm 113:3 "From the rising of the sun unto the going down of the same the LORD'S name *is* to be praised."

Rejoice because I am redeemed.

Psalm 71:23 "My lips shall greatly rejoice when I sing unto thee; and my soul, which thou hast redeemed."

Rejoice because He is trustworthy, and I choose to trust Him.

Psalm 13:5 "But I have trusted in thy mercy; my heart shall rejoice in thy salvation."

Rejoice because praise is beautiful.

Psalm 33:1 "Rejoice in the LORD, O ye righteous: *for* praise is comely for the upright."

Chapter Five

Think on These Things

Philippians 4:8 "Finally, brethren, whatsoever things are true, whatsoever things *are* honest, whatsoever things *are* just, whatsoever things *are* pure, whatsoever things *are* lovely, whatsoever things *are* of good report; if *there be* any virtue, and if *there be* any praise, think on these things."

The book of Philippians is a book about rejoicing. In verse 4, Paul told them to rejoice alway. Now he is telling them *how* to rejoice. Verse 6 tells them to be careful (full of care) for nothing, but to pray with thanksgiving. Now he comes to the end of his letter to them, and says, "Finally, brethren..." and he tells them what to think about.

When my dad taught me to drive, he told me to always focus on where I was going and check things like speed, traffic, signs, etc. "You will always go where you focus. If you focus on the ditch, you will end up in the ditch. If you focus on oncoming traffic, you will drive into it. Check everything. Focus on where you need to go." In life, where we focus our mind is where our life will go. What do you think about the most?

The Bible has a lot to say about thoughts, both man's and God's.

> Matthew 22:37-40 "Jesus said unto him, Thou shalt love the Lord thy God with all thy heart, and with all thy soul, and with all thy mind. [38]This is the first and great commandment. [39]And the second *is* like unto it, Thou shalt love thy neighbour as thyself. [40]On these two commandments hang all the law and the prophets."

Mark 12:30-31 and Luke 10:27 are sister passages to this. God commands us to love the Lord with everything we are—including our mind. It's very hard to love the Lord with all our minds when we are thinking about the wrong things.

> Romans 12:1-2 "I beseech you therefore, brethren, by the mercies of God, that ye present your bodies a living sacrifice, holy, acceptable unto God, *which is* your reasonable service. [2]And be not conformed to this world: **but be ye transformed by the renewing of your mind**, that ye may prove what *is* that good, and acceptable, and perfect, will of God."

How can we present our bodies as living sacrifices and be holy and acceptable to God if we clutter our minds with self-centered thoughts and the things of the world? Remember, you will go the direction you think.

If our minds are not where they should be, what can we do? We shouldn't throw our hands up in despair and say, "I can't do it!" Paul gives hope and instruction, "…be ye transformed by the renewing of your mind."

Renewing means making new again, repairing, re-establishing, reviving. We are human and it is natural to get our minds focused on, and cluttered with, the wrong things. We are told to be transformed by the renewing of our mind. Renewing our minds transforms us back to a living sacrifice, holy, acceptable unto God.

Sometimes our focus isn't so much worldly as it is self-focused. "Why is this happening to me? How could they do this to me? Why doesn't God fix my situation or give me the blessing I long for?" When we allow our thoughts to go in this direction, we turn inward, thinking more of ourselves, nursing our hurts. Notice each of these questions focuses on me. This is often our natural response to trouble, but God doesn't want us to behave naturally. We are supposed to bring our thoughts into submission to God.

Either Satan plants these thoughts or they are a natural by-product of sinful flesh. Whether we have deep wounds or disappointments and unmet expectations, dwelling on them causes them to fester. They become breeding grounds for unforgiveness, bitterness, discontent, and many other sins. They cripple and destroy. There is no peace when we dwell on hurts—past or present, real or imagined.

> 2 Corinthians 10:4-5 "(For the weapons of our warfare *are* not carnal, but mighty through God to the pulling down of strong holds;) ⁵Casting down imaginations, and every high thing that exalteth itself against the knowledge of God, and bringing into captivity every thought to the obedience of Christ;"

Another common response to trouble I see in counseling ladies is the tendency to use imagination to escape temporarily from our sorrow. When we escape into a fantasy where we control what happens, we are not thinking about things that are true and honest. Sometimes, these fantasies are not pure or lovely either. We must bring these thoughts into obedience to Christ.

I would like us to look again at the following verse.

> Isaiah 26:3 "Thou wilt keep him in perfect peace, whose mind is stayed on thee: because he trusteth in thee."

Every time I have allowed my mind to focus on my trials instead of God, His goodness, and His power, I struggled with anxiety, anger, discouragement, bitterness, or depression. However, when I faced the hardest trials with my mind fixed on God,

I walked through the valley with peace, joy, courage, and contentment. These valleys have included not only the miscarriages and chronic, debilitating illness but also betrayal with personal attacks, death of a loved one, and more. God can give victory in **any** situation when we obey Him and keep our minds focused on Him.

Have you ever wondered why some people become bitter and angry in trials, while others grow sweeter and more gracious? Why do some talk of God's faithfulness, goodness, and their blessings while others talk about their hurts, disappointments, inconveniences, or trouble? I believe this is the key to which kind of person you become through trials: fixing your focus. I became that bitter, angry person until I learned these lessons.

When you find life off-kilter, when you dwell on the hurts, when you find you're not as close to God as you once were, it is time to renew your mind and readjust your focus. He promises perfect peace to those who keep their mind stayed on Him. I have proved this verse. Every time I don't have peace, my focus is on the wrong things. When I fix my heart and mind on Him, peace returns.

Chapter Six

Battle for the Mind

Isaiah 26:3 "Thou wilt keep *him* in perfect peace,
whose mind *is* stayed *on thee:* because he trusteth in thee."

One of our greatest battles during trials is the battle for our minds. If the enemy can get you to believe lies, focus on the wrong things, and mess with your mind, he has won a significant part of the battle. *Our thoughts drive our emotions and actions.* We often think our emotions are driving our thoughts, but that's not true. Let me repeat this important truth. Our thoughts drive our emotions and actions, not the other way around.

Here is an excerpt from a journal entry I later used in a blog post:

> I am so drained today. This is not the fatigue of a day's work well done, but bone-deep weariness, a crushing fatigue that has lingered for weeks. It is present when I wake and overwhelming as the day ends. It is a fatigue that makes it difficult to accomplish my simple work.

Cooking dinner is a struggle, and washing dishes afterward is sometimes impossible. Tiredness this deep causes the mind to wander places it usually doesn't go.

When you struggle with infertility, it is easy to view every part of life through that lens. Today I viewed this fatigue through that same lens. What if God gave us a child? Would I even be strong enough to care for them the way I should and still take care of the house? Forget the typesetting and printing for ministry here; could I do the basics? How would I ever make it when motherhood is challenging to the youngest, most energetic ladies? Then the enemy whispers, "He could have (should have) already healed you. Then it wouldn't be an issue."

Satan is called our enemy for a reason: an enemy is against you. They want nothing good for you and fight for your downfall, your lack of peace, and your pain. Enemies get joy from any evil that befalls you. Your pain is their great triumph. That is what Satan is to us. He fights against us, and he so often uses our own minds to bring the worst pain. He uses our pain to turn us against the only One who can bring comfort and healing to our spirits. And often we let him without even a fight.

Isaiah 26:3 is a critical reminder to us to keep our mind stayed on the Lord and trust Him.

Webster's 1828 dictionary defines *stayed* as fixed, settled, sober. Our mind must stay fixed and settled on God. There is no peace when we focus on ourselves or our trials. The only path to peace is keeping our minds stayed on God, trusting in Him. I can always tell when my focus is wrong because my peace flees.

Matthew 22:37-38 "Jesus said unto him, Thou shalt love the Lord thy God with all thy heart, and with all thy soul, and with all thy mind. [38]This is the first and great commandment."

Verse 37 tells us how to love God, including with the mind. Verse 38 tells us it is a commandment, not a suggestion. Satan wants to sidetrack us and derail us. His best tool is getting us into wrong thinking patterns. If he can get us believing his lies, our actions follow. This was his plan of attack in the garden with Eve. It was effective then, and he still uses it today. There is only one way to win this battle: focus on God, love Him, and trust Him. We don't naturally do this. It is a choice.

When Satan is bombarding us with lies or the temptation to focus on ourselves, this can seem an impossible battle to win. I'd like to share some weapons that helped me win this battle.

1. **The Word of God.** Nothing wins this battle faster than truth. Hold each thought up to Scripture and see how it stands. Does it line up with the Word of God? If it doesn't, reject it and cling to the truth, even if the thought *feels* true. Read and meditate on verses that show God's character. If it is a lie that you often entertain, write it down, and write truths from God's Word to combat the lie.

2. **Praise.** God delights in our praise and it changes us. Praise diverts our focus from ourselves and our trouble, putting it back on the One who deserves it. Psalm 22:3 says God inhabits praise. We can praise God through prayer, writing, singing, or telling someone else how good God has been to us.

Praise can be hard when life is in shambles. Corrie Ten Boom told the story of being moved to a barracks in the concentration camp and finding it infested with fleas. It was the last straw for Corrie. Nazis had invaded their beloved homeland, killing people they knew and loved. The Nazis arrested Corrie and her family for helping Jews escape terrible persecution and death. Their captors took Corrie's 100-year-old father and brother to another camp, and they worried about their father. Now, they had to live with fleas.

Corrie's sister, Betsie, challenged her to praise God even for the fleas. Corrie struggled with that, but eventually praised God even for the fleas, although she didn't understand why God allowed them. She didn't feel glad for them. She obeyed, regardless of feelings. Corrie later learned that the guards never stopped their Bible studies or bothered them in their barracks because they knew about the fleas. While the fleas seemed like

35

the last straw in a horrific situation, they were actually God's loving protection. Try praising God for what He is doing in your situation, even when you don't understand it. The only wise God knows what He is doing.[2]

3. **Music**. This ties in with praise. Don't listen to mournful music that will help you wallow. It is tempting to play the songs that focus on trials. Play, sing, or listen to music that puts your focus on God's goodness, faithfulness, and power. If you like classical music, try listening to composers like Bach and Handel, men who praised God through their music.

4. **Remember**. Remember God's faithfulness and answers to prayer in the past. Let your mind travel to Bible stories that show God's power and grace. Think back to the times He has worked in your life. Remember, His ways are not our ways, and He doeth all things well.

I'd like to close this chapter with the final thoughts in that journal entry. By redirecting my mind, I won the battle that day and regained the peace I had lost.

> So, although I'm too tired to fight today, I'll stand firm by rejecting those sad thoughts and focusing on the blessings God has given me. During these times, His amazing grace is enough to keep me singing. His peace, amid tremendous heartache, is enough to keep me loving Him. His power is enough to keep me trusting that nothing is too hard for Him. His unfailing love is enough to remind me He wants what is best for me. If that best comes only through pain, He loves me enough to allow the pain. What more could I ask? So, with a weary body but encouraged spirit, I can face the rest of my day. As I go, I remind myself that He doeth all things well.

How will you win the battle today? What lies will you reject and what truth will you choose to ponder?

---

[2] Corrie Ten Boom. (1971) 2006. *The Hiding Place*. 35th Anniversary Edition, Kindle. Chosen Books.

Chapter Seven

Turn Your Eyes Upon Jesus

Hebrews 12:2 "Looking unto Jesus the author and finisher of *our* faith; who for the joy that was set before him endured the cross, despising the shame, and is set down at the right hand of the throne of God."

Based on a post from December 22, 2015

Thanksgiving is past and Christmas is almost upon us. For most of my life, this was my favorite time of year. Thanksgiving was our favorite family holiday. Christmas was a time for family, fellowship, special services at church, remembering God's greatest gift to us, and, of course, lots of lovely food for both holidays.

Our first holiday season after we married was wonderful. We weren't close enough to our families to join them, but we enjoyed our time together and with my former church in Texas. By our first Christmas, I was expecting. Other than not being able to deal with the meat because of nausea, it was perfect.

By the next Thanksgiving and Christmas, everything had changed. I had miscarried 3 times, the third just days before Thanksgiving. That week, I went through the motions, enjoying family and being thankful for all of God's blessings and the gift of Jesus Christ, but part of me was empty.

I thought it was because the loss was so fresh, and the wound was still open. Since then, I have learned that it's not just the newness of the wound that causes this. Each year has been the same. We spent the next two Thanksgivings with my family and Christmases with Rob's family. We had good food, great fellowship, and loved being with family after months away on deputation, but part of my heart wasn't in it. It was seeing shadows of what might have been. In my heart, I saw each little one we had said goodbye to. I knew how old they would be, if they would have been nursing, eating mashed potatoes, or gnawing on turkey, or if they were due just days after the holiday. In my heart, I saw their eyes light up with the festivities; I saw myself slipping into the bedroom to put them down for their nap, and their grandparents' joy and delight in meeting them. But it was all dreams and wishes. None of them were there.

We now have 6 babies in heaven, none with us. Thanksgiving was bittersweet our first year on the mission field together. We spent the week with friends. We had sweet fellowship, lots of good food, and a great Thanksgiving service. I enjoyed their children, but everywhere I looked, I ached at what might have been, but wasn't.

Over the last few days, I've been moping. That's the only word for it. I've carried on with the work I need to do. We've been planning for our upcoming move, measuring for curtains, finding fabric stores, doing Bible studies, planning the week's menu and Christmas dinner, and all the other things we do each day. But my heart hasn't been in it.

Through all the work and planning, I've been seeing shadows of "maybes" and "should/would have beens". Which room would have been a nursery, which baby would have been big enough to prod us to decorate for Christmas, even though we're moving just days after, which baby would have been still too little to notice, and the baby that would be due in just a couple of months. In the middle of that is the wonder if we'll ever have a child. I'm now 45. There's a strong possibility that I won't have children. So I've been moping. Might as well call it what it is.

But this morning, again, the Lord is drawing me out of the mopes. He's reminding me that keeping my eyes on my losses (babies and dreams) keeps me down, but keeping my eyes on Him lifts me up. It's really my choice whether I have a blessed Christmas or a sad one. Yes, the ache of losing a child is always with me, but I can choose not to dwell on the pain and loss. I can thank God that I was privileged to carry them for even that short time. One day, I will see them in Heaven. I can thank God for an amazing and supportive husband. Truthfully, I can thank God for so many things.

The loss and ache are always there, but they can take a back seat to the joy that God gives when I choose to praise, rejoice, and keep my eyes fixed firmly on Him. I can look at the waves and wind, and sink like Peter did. Or I can keep my eyes firmly on my Saviour and walk with Him amid any storm or heartache. The choice is mine. So today I chose to stop moping. When the memories and heartache comes, I choose to thank God for His manifold blessings and rejoice in this season.

Philippians 4:6-8 "Be careful for nothing; but in every thing by prayer and supplication with thanksgiving let your requests be made known unto God. [7]And the peace of God, which passeth all understanding, shall keep your hearts and minds through Christ Jesus. [8]Finally, brethren, whatsoever things are true, whatsoever things *are* honest, whatsoever things *are* just, whatsoever things *are* pure, whatsoever things *are* lovely, whatsoever things *are* of good report; if *there be* any virtue, and if *there be* any praise, think on these things."

May God give you peace and joy in this Christmas season, no matter what heartache, what loss, what grief you bear. Because peace on earth (or in our hearts) can only come from the Prince of Peace. Comfort can only come from the Comforter. Only He can give joy out of sorrow and peace out of turmoil. May the Prince of Peace reign in your heart today.

As embarrassing as it is to post my failings and my moping (I'm grown up now; I shouldn't act like a child), I choose to share, anyway. Because if it encourages just one person to find joy amid sorrow by reading about my failings and my God's faithfulness, it's worth it.

I wrote the above post in 2015. We just celebrated Christmas of 2023 as I work on the second draft of this book. I want to testify to God's goodness in the past years. We didn't have more children. I still miss our babies, and holidays have a hint of sadness as I think of what might have been, but it's only the faintest hint, when I keep my focus on God and His goodness, not the crushing burden and dark shadow it was. This year was also our first Christmas without my dad. He went Home to Heaven in February. Yes, there were some tears, but learning to focus on

God and His goodness helped me through this loss, too. We had a sweet Christmas season.

However, if I focus on the loss, the pain and ache grow and my joy dims. If you are facing this, please fight the battle to keep your focus on the Lord and reasons for gratitude. Praise Him in the dark, trusting He will bring back light. This was the path to my healing. If I forsake it, I find myself back in the shadows. Keep your focus and faith in God so you can keep your peace and joy.

Chapter Eight

Peace in Pain

2 Peter 1:2-3 "Grace and peace be multiplied unto you through the knowledge of God and of Jesus our Lord, ³According as his divine power hath given unto us all things that *pertain* unto life and godliness, through the knowledge of him that hath called us to glory and virtue."

Are you struggling to find peace in this season of life? That was my biggest struggle through the years of illness, miscarriages, infertility, and disappointments. How do I find lasting peace? It would come, then it would go. What was wrong that I couldn't have consistent peace? I am learning what brings peace and what chases it away. Today, I would like to share some of what I have learned with you.

I have read or heard the verses above hundreds of times, but I never realized fully what they were saying until I was going through a Bible study[3] with a young lady several years ago. This grace and peace that Peter wants his readers to have comes **through the knowledge of God and Jesus**! I don't know why it took me so long to see it. We long for peace in the middle of overwhelming pain or grief. We know life will never be the same. Sometimes the pain overwhelms us and seems to drive peace away. Truthfully, grief doesn't chase away my peace. My peace flees when I reject the truth about God and Jesus, choosing to believe lies. As I meditate on truth, grow in my knowledge of God, He pours out His grace and peace reigns.

Meditate. For some, the word conjures up images of sitting cross-legged on the ground, eyes closed, and fingers in a funny position. Meditation simply means to mull things over, to chew on them. I've had ladies tell me they can't meditate because of stress or brain fog. But then I usually ask, "Do you think about this problem, examine it from all angles, think about possible (negative) outcomes, chew on it?" They almost always answer, "Yes." When we do this, we're meditating on the problem. Now we just need to turn it around and meditate on the truth. Consider what God says about it. Chew on it. Examine it from all angles. Now you're meditating on the right thing instead of the wrong things.

Meditate on the Right things

> 1 Timothy 4:15-16 "Meditate on these things; give thyself wholly to them; that thy profiting may appear to all. [16]Take heed unto thyself, and unto the doctrine; continue in them: for in doing this thou shalt both save thyself, and them that hear thee."

Paul told Timothy that when he meditates on the truths written here, and gives himself wholly to them, there will be a visible change in him: "...that thy profiting may appear to all." Meditating on truth will bring peace and change us so completely that people will see the difference in us.

---

[3] Berg, Jim. 2005. *Quieting a Noisy Soul Kit*. Greenville, SC: BJU Press.

44

While I was going through the six miscarriages and the secondary infertility, there were many times that I got my focus off of God and my peace fled. At one time, I wondered why I sometimes had peace, but I couldn't hang on to it consistently. It turns out it all boils down to my focus: what do I meditate on? When I meditated on what others had, what I had lost, the disappointments, the pain, or the hardships, peace fled. When I meditated on these things, I believed Satan's lies. However, when I meditated on God, His character, His faithfulness, His power, His wisdom, His greatness, and when I grew in my knowledge of Him, peace reigned and there was sufficient grace to carry the load of grief or pain. The burden truly seemed light. The difference was not the weight of the pain or grief. It was what I believed and meditated upon. I proved this to be true in the valleys that followed too.

Counting Your Blessings

One of the many things we can meditate on when we struggle is our blessings. This is sometimes hard. When faced with trials, the enemy tempts us to count our problems instead of our blessings. The litany of woes runs through our head, and our heart focuses on them. Try turning that around and listing your blessings.

> When upon life's billows you are tempest-tossed,
> When you are discouraged, thinking all is lost,
> Count your many blessings, name them one by one,
> And it will surprise you what the Lord has done.
>
> Count your blessings, name them one by one,
> Count your blessings, see what God has done!
> Count your blessings, name them one by one,
> Count your many blessings, see what God hath done.[4]

This song has often realigned my thinking and recalibrated my heart, bringing me back to praising God.

---

[4] Oatman, Jr, Johnson. 1897. *Count Your Blessings*. https://library.timelesstruths.org/music/Count_Your_Blessings/.

Ephesians 1:3 "Blessed *be* the God and Father of our Lord Jesus Christ, who hath blessed us with all spiritual blessings in heavenly *places* in Christ:"

God has blessed us abundantly. If He never gave us anything beyond eternal life, we would have nothing to complain about. Yet He *daily* loadeth us with benefits, according to Psalm 68:19. If you are struggling to count your blessings, start with Calvary and your salvation. Our greatest blessing is the reconciliation to God through salvation.

Place of Peace

During this past Christmas season, one of our pastors brought a message on peace. He said something I don't remember ever hearing. Peace, at least in the passages he was sharing, primarily means "to join" or "set at one again". Our peace comes from being joined to, at one with, Christ. Our peace is found in His presence.

One day, we will be at perfect, eternal peace in His presence in Heaven. But we don't have to wait until eternity to have peace. Until God calls us Home, our solace and comfort comes in lingering in His presence and resting in Him as we trust Him to do great and mighty things, even if they're not what we wished for.

Psalm 91:2-4 "I will say of the LORD, *He is* my refuge and my fortress: my God; in him will I trust. 3Surely he shall deliver thee from the snare of the fowler, *and* from the noisome pestilence. ⁴He shall cover thee with his feathers, and under his wings shalt thou trust: his truth *shall be thy* shield and buckler."

Give up your burdens and desires to Him. He will sustain you.

Psalm 55:22 "Cast thy burden upon the LORD, and he shall sustain thee: he shall never suffer the righteous to be moved."

Chapter Nine

It's Not About Me

1 Corinthians 6:19-20 "What? know ye not that your body is the temple of the Holy Ghost which is in you, which ye have of God, and ye are not your own? [20]For ye are bought with a price: therefore glorify God in your body, and in your spirit, which are God's."

When we go through trials, especially long, drawn out ones, it is easy to let them fill our vision until we can see nothing else. If we let it, our trouble will consume our time, energy, thoughts, and conversation. Our eyes turn inward instead of staying upward.

One thing God taught me through trials is that nothing in this life is about me. It is such an important truth that I share it with everyone God allows me to study with. Nothing in my life is about me. I am bought with a price, so I belong to Him. That means everything in my life is about the One who bought me.

The first time I came face-to-face with this truth was on our first anniversary. When you're a missionary, and you get married in the middle of mission conference season, you can expect your anniversaries to be affected. I never even thought of this until my husband told me he scheduled us to be at a missions conference on our first anniversary. It wasn't a problem. We were missionaries, so it was to be expected.

We arrived at our destination and discovered we were staying with a family in the church, along with two other couples. Everyone had a great time that week. We enjoyed the conference at church and the fellowship at home. I got to meet a dear family that I had typeset for, but never met. I loved it. There was just one fly in the ointment. Sharing a house with 3 other couples was not the romantic vision I had in my mind for our first anniversary. I had expected to enjoy everyone at the conference and meals, then have somewhere to get away alone together the rest of the time. I was basing my expectations solely on previous experience.

To say it disappointed me would be an understatement. Every other day was wonderful, but on our anniversary, I struggled. As I prayed (complained to God), He started working on me concerning this concept. It's not about me. I knew my life overall belonged to Him. Hadn't I surrendered to go anywhere He sent? I had surrendered to His will when he took my 3 babies (at that time) to Heaven. Wasn't my anniversary something that could be about me, about us?

The answer is no. And we find the reason in our verse. I am bought with a price. That means I do not belong to myself. I belong to God. If I belong to Him, everything in my life is to be about Him. He is the reason I live. Everything about my life is for His glory. If I must suffer hard trials or minor inconveniences to be refined and made more like Him, then I need to submit to it with grace and trust.

Besides the refining that I undergo when I submit to trials, I never know when God orchestrates or allows problems, disappointments, or delays to put me in the path of someone who needs to hear about Him. Am I willing to give up my hopes, dreams, ease, or anything else to be used completely by God?

D.L. Moody once heard evangelist Henry Varley say, "The world has yet to see what God can do through a man who is totally yielded to Him." Mr. Moody set out to be that man, and God used him greatly. If Jesus has bought us with His blood and we belong to Him, should we not set out to be fully and wholly consecrated?

I wish I could say I live this. I am working on it, but I forget too often. Yet, when I remember that not one bit of this life is about me, I have peace and joy instead of stress. My life is about my God. It's about loving Him, loving others, and being used as He chooses.

The only way I know to do this is to follow the advice of the beloved hymn, "Turn Your Eyes Upon Jesus."*[5]

> O soul, are you weary and troubled?
> No light in the darkness you see?
> There's light for a look at the Savior,
> And life more abundant and free!
> Turn your eyes upon Jesus,
> Look full in His wonderful face,
> And the things of earth will grow strangely dim,
> In the light of His glory and grace.

Every time I follow this advice, I find peace and contentment, regardless of the circumstances. We have the perfect example of this in Jesus. He was born in what the world considered dubious circumstances. The people He came to save despised, rejected, betrayed, mocked, and killed Him. Yet we see in Hebrews that He endured it all for the joy that was set before Him.

Hebrews 12:2 "Looking unto Jesus the author and finisher of our faith; who for the joy that was set before him endured the cross, despising the shame, and is set down at the right hand of the throne of God.

---

[5] Lemmel, Helen H. 1922. *Turn Your Eyes upon Jesus.* http://library. timelesstruths.org/music/Turn_Your_Eyes_upon_Jesus.

We too have a joy set before us, and this verse tells us how to run this race the way we should. Looking unto Jesus—that's the key. It's not about me, it's all about Him. If I keep my eyes on Him, it is harder to lose sight of that truth. When the enemy comes and whispers how unfair or hard life is, I can keep, or regain, my peace by turning my eyes away from the trial and keep them focused on the One who went to the cross for me.

Although He is the Creator of all things, He came to die, so I might live. When I remember this, nothing is too hard to endure.

One of the sweetest things about surrender is how God works in our lives, not always as we expected, but as He knows is best for us. God restored my peace when I surrendered to His plan, but He also gave an unexpected blessing. The afternoon of our anniversary, one of the senior missionaries staying with us stopped my husband and slipped some money in his hand and told him to take me out for a nice dinner alone. While we did not have the anniversary I expected, we had a sweet time together before returning to the encouraging fellowship at the house. I am learning to always trust God's plan and let go of my expectations.

Chapter Ten

Purpose in Pain

Romans 8:28 "And we know that all things work together for good to them that love God, to them who are the called according to *his* purpose."

We looked at this verse in the last chapter. When we read verses like this, we often want to know what good God will bring from our pain. How can any good come from the loss of a child or spouse, lost jobs, chronic illness, betrayal, failure, or any other trial we are facing? We would all like to find the purpose in our pain, to know that some good is coming from this heartache or trial.

Some people get to see the good immediately. They see people saved, wandering children returned to God and the family. Great things happen. We love these stories. However, some of us never see what God is doing behind the scenes, but if we look closely, we can see what God is doing in us when we submit to the trials He allows in our lives. One day, we will see the complete picture.

I love the story of Job. I always walk away from Job's story with something I had never noticed before. Recently I was reading it again. In an amazingly short period of time, Job lost nearly everything. He lost his children, wealth, health, influence, and standing in the community. His children are dead. He has no stock or servants left. His health is gone and in its place is the pain of disgusting boils. His wife is so overwhelmed with her grief, she challenges him to curse God and die. When it seems he can endure no more, his friends come to comfort him and end up blaming him for his trials, accusing him of hidden sin. How much can one man endure? What good could come from all of this?

In the beginning, we see Job standing strong. He blesses the name of the Lord when the whirlwind kills his children, and bandits steal his wealth and kill his servants.

> Job 1:20-21 "Then Job arose, and rent his mantle, and shaved his head, and fell down upon the ground, and worshipped, [21]And said, Naked came I out of my mother's womb, and naked shall I return thither: the LORD gave, and the LORD hath taken away; blessed be the name of the LORD."

When he loses his health and his wife breaks under the pressure, He speaks only confidence in God's goodness.

> Job 2:9-10 "Then said his wife unto him, Dost thou still retain thine integrity? curse God, and die. [10]But he said unto her, Thou speakest as one of the foolish women speaketh. What? shall we receive good at the hand of God, and shall we not receive evil? In all this did not Job sin with his lips."

When Job voices his grief and his friends turn on him, he declares, "Though he slay me, yet will I trust in him…" (13:15). As time passes and his friends don't let up, his health doesn't improve, his grief is still as overwhelming, we see Job get a bit discouraged. In chapter 6, he wishes God would destroy him. Chapter 10 records his cry for God to show him why He has brought such sorrow on him as he recounts what this trial has done to him.

Even in his discouragement and despair, Job tells his unhelpful friends that when God has tried him, he shall come forth as gold. Yet he cries out against the change in his life: the friends who judge him, those who despise him, his sorrow and pain. He recalls his life and good works, describes the agony of his current situation. There seems to be no hope, no purpose, no relief in sight.

Then God speaks

Ah, when we hear the voice of God in the midst of our pain, everything changes. The circumstances may not change, but our perspective and focus changes, and this makes all the difference. God reminds Job of who He is. He is the One who laid the foundations of the earth, sets the boundaries of the seas, causes it to rain, sends lightning, hunts prey for the lions, provides for the raven, commands the eagle to mount and make her nest on high. He reveals His might and character to Job. Amid his crushing sorrow, Job finally sees God for who He truly is. Job served God, prayed, sacrificed, and walked in God's way. Yet Job seems to have only had a limited understanding of who God is because at the end of this valley Job declares in Job 42:5, "I have heard of thee by the hearing of the ear: but now mine eye seeth thee." Through Job's greatest pain came his greatest blessing: truly knowing God. We looked at this in "Peace in Your Pain". Peace comes in our knowledge of God. Job discovered this.

My husband and I talked about adoption when we realized I probably would not carry a baby to term. I wanted to adopt, but we didn't have a home. We were on deputation, preparing to move to Africa, living in missions apartments. We didn't know of anyone who would let us adopt a child in our circumstances, so we prayed and put it in God's hands.

The opportunity to adopt never arose in Africa. There were many orphans in part of the country where we lived, but the first choice for adoption was always an African family. We never had peace about pursuing it, believing God wanted us to wait and rest in Him. If He wanted us to adopt, He would bring us a child.

Just before we went to Brazil in 2021, an opportunity literally dropped into our laps. Hours after buying our plane tickets, someone called and asked if we were willing to adopt. They knew a little boy who needed a family. Emotions and thoughts swirled through our hearts and minds like a dust storm on a Texas plain. We said we would pray. The next day, she sent a picture of this little man and we immediately loved him. We asked close family and our pastors to pray with us.

The next day, we told them we would love to meet him and his legal guardians[6] as long as they understood we were on our way to Brazil. They knew we were missionaries and were fine with that in theory, but that's a far cry from knowing we had tickets to leave soon. She said she would let them know we had tickets to go later that year. Three days later, my heart broke as I read the words, "(Guardian) seems very against him moving so far away. I'm really sorry. I'll let you know if there are any changes."

Rob and I prayed and talked it over. We both knew God had led us to Brazil and we could not turn our backs on, or delay obeying, God's leading, not even if it meant losing the opportunity to be parents. So, we prayed and vowed again to follow God, regardless of the cost, and trust Him to sort out our lives according to His plan. With heavy (but peaceful) hearts, we continued to plan our trip to Brazil. There was no change of heart or mind. We flew to Brazil without the son we hoped would go with us.

The following days and weeks gave me ample opportunity to practice the sacrifice of praise and thanksgiving. My heart ached, and the enemy capitalized on that. It was a daily, hourly, and often moment-by-moment battle to keep my focus on God and His goodness instead of the pain of this devastating loss. Satan tried to convince us that the cost was too great, but praising God through the tears and pain kept me settled and focused.

---

[6] I am keeping this vague to protect the privacy of everyone involved.

The next few months were a roller coaster. While waiting for our permits to be processed, the airline canceled our tickets without notice. The consulate lost our permit applications. Despite the receipt they generated when we submitted them, they had no record of ever receiving them. Then my brother-in-law passed away and Mom and I flew to Alaska to be with my sister and her kids. At that moment, I was thankful for all the delays so I could be with her.

Finally, we learned we could apply for our permits from within Brazil, so we bought tickets again, gathered basic belongings and two boxes of literature, and headed to Brazil, knowing we could stay six months, but unsure of anything beyond that.

Every delay in getting to Brazil and getting visas to stay, the enemy reminded me of what we had given up to get there and asked if it was worth it. The answer is a resounding yes. Regardless of the cost, following God's plan for our lives is always worth it.

We still do not know why God brought this possibility into our lives, knowing we could not adopt this child and still follow His leading to Brazil. We didn't see great things accomplished while we were there, and we only got to stay for a year. But we know God had a purpose, and we trust Him to accomplish it, even if we can't see what it is. We also know God can bring the increase from seed planted and watered long after we are gone.

Do you want to find a purpose in your pain? Find God. Don't just rely on the knowledge of your salvation, or what you've learned of Him up to this point. Seek Him. Meditate on Him and who He is. In knowing God, we find purpose. Maybe knowing God more will be all the purpose you discover until God reveals everything in Heaven. It may be from your pain God brings great blessing, ministry, and purpose that you will see in this life. For Job, he knew God like he had never known Him before and God restored his wealth, reputation, influence, and gave him more children. Yet I can't help feeling that even if God had restored none of these things, Job would have been content in this new understanding of the God he had served.

Today, as I work on this chapter again, my heart hurts. The enemy whispers it's too hard to share, just leave it out. But what if the purpose of my pain is to encourage someone and give them hope to keep going? It is worth reliving the pain if it encourages one person to keep trusting God.

> 2 Corinthians 1:3-4 "Blessed *be* God, even the Father of our Lord Jesus Christ, the Father of mercies, and the God of all comfort; [4]Who comforteth us in all our tribulation, that we may be able to comfort them which are in any trouble, by the comfort wherewith we ourselves are comforted of God."

The peace and joy that God gives when I rest in His perfect knowledge and goodness overwhelms this temporary pain. I know He is working good through this and that is always worth it.

> Psalm 119:71 "It is good *for me* that I have been afflicted; that I might learn thy statutes."

Chapter Eleven

When God Doesn't Deliver

Psalm 34:17 "The righteous cry, and the Lord heareth, and delivereth them out of all their troubles."

This was my verse of the day and my daily Bible reading was in Esther, so I considered Psalm 34:17 in light of what I was reading. I know we have mentioned Esther, but I would like to examine her story more closely to see what we can learn.

Esther probably prayed not to be taken when the decree went out to gather all the beautiful virgins for the king. I'm sure Mordecai prayed for God to deliver her, too. Esther had no way of knowing what deliverance God had in mind when He allowed the king's men to take her from her home. Where was this great God she heard of from childhood? He had delivered with mighty power many times: the Red Sea parting, the crumbling walls of Jericho, and more. Could He, would He, hide one beautiful Jewish girl from the king's men? Yes, He could. No, He would not.

If she had to be taken for this grotesque and vile pageant, she could pray the king found his bride and she would never be called on. She could never go home again, never marry or have children, but she could live in relative safety in the house of women.

After a year of mandatory purification and beauty treatments, Esther's hopes crumbled as Hegai, keeper of the women, sent her to spend the night with the king. This wicked Gentile king would use a pure, innocent, Jewish girl and probably forget about her, leaving her humbled and forever in the house of the concubines. Why didn't God answer her prayers? Why didn't He answer Mordecai's prayers?

Then the improbable happened. The king chose Esther to be his queen. We have no record of how she felt about it. She may have been excited or filled with dread. She couldn't move to the house of concubines, hoping the king forgot her and never called again. Esther would be in the palace, surrounded by heathen things, required to eat unclean food because she couldn't reveal she was a Jewess.

This was not a "happily ever after" fairy tale romance. Yes, she had luxury, but not the life all Jewish girls dreamed of. This king was no prince charming. He had ordered his servants to parade his last wife before his drunken guests so he could show off her beauty. She could not expect tenderness or protection from such a man.

This was a man who chose his new queen bride by spending each night with a different, beautiful woman and choosing the one who pleased him most. He was unconcerned that he had destroyed the hopes and lives of so many young ladies. This is Esther's reality when Haman sets out to destroy the Jews and Mordecai tells her to reveal her Jewish heritage and beg for their lives.

In chapter 4, we see Esther fears her husband and doesn't have a close relationship with him. He hasn't sent for her in 30 days. She can't just bring this up one night at family dinner. Appearing before her husband without an invitation can cost her life. This is a genuine fear, causing her to ask not only Morde-cai, but all the Jews in Shushan, to fast and pray with her for 3 days before she risks her life. Apparently, this was not an ob-scure law, but one her husband used often enough to make it a genuine threat.

What must have been running through Esther's mind as she prepared herself to approach the king? God had not delivered her from the king's men when they rounded up the virgins. He hadn't spared her from being sent to the king for his pleasure. Would His answer be "no" this time too?

Sometimes God says "no" to our requests, so we believe Sa-tan's lies. He tells us that God doesn't care about us, we're not good enough, God will always tell us "no," or another of his many lies. Before long, we expect God to answer all our prayers with a "no." Like Esther, we cannot see what God is doing. We don't realize that His "no" to some prayers is because He has a greater "yes" and a bigger plan.

As Esther prayed, stood trembling before the king, suffered Haman's pathetic pleas, and awaited the king's decision, she did not know how great God's "yes" was going to be. Only after her years of no's and suffering could she look back and see God's hand. Every "no" had been working toward this amazing deliverance.

We read Esther's story in a few chapters, considering all Scripture and history. Esther lived years with all the "no's", ig-norant of the great deliverance God was preparing. God didn't deliver her from the king or his men because He had a bigger plan, but she didn't know this while she suffered.

Jesus was told "no" as well. Many of the people He came to deliver told Him no, but that didn't hurt as much as what was to come. After being rejected, He faced the garden of Gethsemane. He prayed, "O my Father, if it be possible, let this cup pass from me..." (Matthew 26:39). God did not answer this prayer with deliverance from the cross. Jesus submitted to the will of the Fa-ther and paid the ultimate sacrifice so we could have the ultimate deliverance.

I encourage you today to shift your focus from God's "no's" to His goodness and power. Trust Him and His promise in Romans 8:28 to work all things together for good. Accept His "no" just as willingly as you accept His "yes." Go beyond accepting it. Thank and praise Him for His "no," trusting that His plan is greater than you can imagine. This is a genuine sacrifice of praise and sacrifice of thanksgiving.

> Psalm 107:21-22 "Oh that men would praise the LORD for his goodness, and for his wonderful works to the children of men! [22]And let them sacrifice the sacrifices of thanksgiving, and declare his works with rejoicing."

God will keep His Word and deliver you in His perfect timing, even if it's a different deliverance than you expect. Trust Him.

Chapter Twelve

When the Enemy Prevails

2 Kings 19:15 "And Hezekiah prayed before the
LORD, and said, O LORD God of Israel, which
dwellest *between* the cherubims, thou art the God, *even*
thou alone, of all the kingdoms of the earth; thou hast
made heaven and earth."

I love the story of Hezekiah, king of Judah. His story is so important, God recorded it three times. I learned much from studying his life. Here we will mostly focus on one episode, but I encourage you to read and study more. You can find his story in 2 Kings 18-20, 2 Chronicles 29-32, and Isaiah 36-39.

Hezekiah was only 25 years old when he began his reign, but God gave him a glowing report. He removed the high places, images, and groves, cleansed the land of idolatry and restored worship of God in the temple. God also records that Hezekiah trusted and clave to the Lord and God was with him and prospered him. He rebelled against Assyria and refused to serve them. Then he smote the Philistines. God was with Hezekiah, and everyone could see it.

In the fourth year of Hezekiah's reign, Assyria went up against Israel, besieging Syria for three years before taking it, and Israel went into captivity because of their sin. Seven years after Israel fell, it was Judah's turn to gain Assyria's attention. At this point, Sennacherib, king of Assyria, has an unbroken track record in battle. Every country Assyria goes up against falls. Not one nation has withstood them. If they don't defeat them on the battlefield, they starve them out in siege, like they did with Samaria.

According to 2 Kings 18, when Sennacherib came against Judah, he took all of their fenced cities. To keep Judah from suffering the same fate as Israel, Hezekiah agreed to pay tribute to Sennacherib. He had to strip the palace and temple of the gold, even scraping it off of the walls and pillars to pay it, but this wasn't enough for Sennacherib. He sent three of his men to Jerusalem to start a demoralizing campaign. They stood in public and taunted Judah with their track record and Hezekiah's supposed weakness—then they maligned God. "No one else's God was big enough to save them. Yours won't be big enough either." In fact, they lie and say God sent them to fight Judah.

I see a progression in how Hezekiah handled the trial of Assyria's invasion. First, he tried to buy favor with Sennacherib. "If I just pay tribute, he'll leave us alone." Often, when trouble comes to our lives, we also try to find a way out of our situation. We look for a reason and a solution.

When that didn't work, Hezekiah went to the house of God, but not before putting on sackcloth and sending a message to the prophet. Maybe I'm reading my past reactions into this passage, but it feels like the message is full of panic.

> 2 Kings 19:3-4 "And they said unto him, Thus saith Hezekiah, This day is a day of trouble, and of rebuke, and blasphemy: for the children are come to the birth, and there is not strength to bring forth. [4]It may be the

LORD thy God will hear all the words of Rabshakeh, whom the king of Assyria his master hath sent to reproach the living God; and will reprove the words which the LORD thy God hath heard: wherefore lift up thy prayer for the remnant that are left."

Isaiah sent God's message of assurance to the king.

2 Kings 19:6-7 "And Isaiah said unto them, Thus shall ye say to your master, Thus saith the LORD, Be not afraid of the words which thou hast heard, with which the servants of the king of Assyria have blasphemed me. ⁷Behold, I will send a blast upon him, and he shall hear a rumour, and shall return to his own land; and I will cause him to fall by the sword in his own land."

As promised, the Assyrians got war news from afar, and prepared to leave for home. After Rabshakeh left, he sent a threatening letter to Hezekiah, promising that this didn't mean deliverance. He had destroyed all the other nations, and he would be back to destroy Judah.

This time, Hezekiah didn't tear his clothes, pull out the sackcloth, or send a panicked message to the prophet. Why? The enemy was still as powerful, their track record still as impressive. What changed? Hezekiah's focus had changed. Armed with God's promise of deliverance, He went to the house of the Lord, spread the threatening letter before God, and prayed. His prayer is a great example for us when we are facing a daunting enemy.

He praised God

2 Kings 19:15 "And Hezekiah prayed before the LORD, and said, O LORD God of Israel, which dwellest between the cherubims, thou art the God, even thou alone, of all the kingdoms of the earth; thou hast made heaven and earth."

Hezekiah began by recognizing who God is: His position and His power. Doing this focuses us on God, seeing His power. Any situation, threat, or person cannot help but shrink when held up to the amazing power of Almighty God. Let that be our first stop when the enemy in our life looks like they are winning. Praise God for who He is, reminding ourselves in the process of how great our God is.

He asked God to see His trouble

> 2 Kings 19:16 "LORD, bow down thine ear, and hear: open, LORD, thine eyes, and see: and hear the words of Sennacherib, which hath sent him to reproach the living God."

He besought God to look at the trouble they were in. And he points out that Sennacherib has not reproached Judah, but God. He has said God isn't big enough to stop him. Hezekiah doesn't hesitate to point this out.

He admitted the enemy is great

> 2 Kings 19:17-18 "Of a truth, LORD, the kings of Assyria have destroyed the nations and their lands, [18]And have cast their gods into the fire: for they were no gods, but the work of men's hands, wood and stone: therefore they have destroyed them."

Hezekiah admits that the enemy is powerful. They do have a track record of success against other nations and lands. Judah is a tiny nation. While still unified, Israel and Judah were a small nation. Now Judah is alone and they are no match for the powerful and ruthless nation of Assyria. Hezekiah admits this to the Lord.

Maybe your enemy is great, and it looks like they have the power to destroy you or part of your life. Admit that to the Lord, remembering that they are more powerful than you, but not more powerful than your God. Too often, we stop at recognizing our weakness and forget to recognize God's power.

He asked for deliverance

> 2 Kings 19:19 "Now therefore, O LORD our God, I beseech thee, save thou us out of his hand, that all the

kingdoms of the earth may know that thou art the
LORD God, even thou only."

Hezekiah's plea for deliverance was not just for Judah's safety and benefit, but that all the nations around would see and know they served the one true God. His plea for deliverance this time was for God to get the glory.

Sometimes our valley holds a powerful enemy, and it looks like they are in control. Never forget, control is an illusion for us. God is the only one in control. Sometimes it looks like the enemy gets the victory, but God is ultimately in control. Other times, like in this story, God shows up and gives a mighty deliverance. Our job is to pray and trust God to do what is right—whether it's delivering us now or saying no—so He can prepare for something greater that we don't see coming.

I want to share a few stories in the Bible that you can read when you face a powerful enemy. These accounts helped me and they will remind you of God's power and control in our lives.

Jesus: The Jews tried to kill Jesus more than once. Yet, they couldn't touch Him until it was His time to die. Rereading the gospels always encourages me.

Job: When God brought Job to Satan's attention, Satan admitted he couldn't touch Job because of God's protection. God gave Satan permission to touch Job's life, but He set boundaries on how far Satan could go. As a child of God, nothing touches me unless God allows it. I can't count how many times this truth encouraged me.

Peter & Paul: There are so many stories about Peter and Paul that illustrate this truth. Sometimes God let their enemies get the upper hand, and sometimes He miraculously delivered them. At all times, God was in control, working in their lives to accomplish His purpose.

Daniel & his three friends: God did not save them from captivity and all they endured as slaves, but He saved them from the sword when the king's wise men didn't know the king's dream and He saved Daniel from the lions. He did not save

Shadrach, Meshach, and Abednego from the furnace, but He saved them from the fire. God chose what could affect Daniel and his friends, what couldn't touch them, and how He would use them for His glory.

What are you facing today? Do you have an enemy trying to destroy your life or family? Are governments trying to keep you from getting visas to spread the gospel? What about someone that makes everything harder and makes you look bad or hinders your progress? Is it a teacher, boss, or other authority that isn't doing right? None of them are in control. God can deliver you, or use you in the trouble you are in.

Whatever you are facing, respond like Hezekiah. Lay it before the Lord. Praise Him. Tell Him that you trust Him and ask for Him to work on your behalf. Then get up and do what is right, trusting God to sort it out His way and in His time.

Remember, God's will is not always humanly fair. Throughout history, we see God's people suffering unfairly while God accomplishes His purpose. Are you willing to submit to the unfairness if God wants to use that to accomplish His will in and through you?

Chapter Thirteen

Envy

Proverbs 27:4 "Wrath *is* cruel, and anger *is* outrageous; but who *is* able to stand before envy?"

One of the greatest temptations in the valley is envy. We see the ease and blessings of others in light of our own troubles, and Satan uses envy to distract and keep us from victory.

The most obvious example of envy I can think of in Scripture is Rachel and Leah. Laban and Jacob made a mess of the lives of these two sisters. Jacob loved Rachel dearly enough to work seven years for her, but Laban tricked Jacob and gave him Leah instead. When Jacob realized Laban had duped him, he bargained to marry Rachel and work seven years for her, too. Being a plural wife would be hard enough, but to put sisters in the position of vying for their husband's attention and affection was terrible, and it bred envy and resentment.

Rachel is the favorite wife, but Leah had children. Leah envies Rachel because Jacob loves her and Rachel envies Leah because she has children. What an unsettled and unhappy family, everyone vying for love, favor, and satisfaction. Each one felt justified in their desire to be loved or have a child. We see the fruit of that envy and strife in their children years later.

It is easy to excuse envy as normal longings or a desire for God's blessings, but we don't do ourselves any favors when we allow envy to infiltrate our lives. Rachel and Leah could have helped each other through their heartache, building a loving and stable home for the children. Instead, they allowed envy to drive a wedge between them.

Somewhere in the middle of our six miscarriages, I let the insidious sin of envy take up residence in my heart. It crept in so slowly and quietly that I didn't realize it was there for too long. I excused it as an honest longing for my children, but it became more than that.

Each time I would see pregnancy or birth announcements, I felt that stab in my heart. I rejoiced for friends and family, but why couldn't I have the same blessing? Why would God withhold the same joy from me? As my health failed, envy showed up in other areas. When I saw older people working and doing more than I could, I wondered why God would let me continually suffer from weakness and debilitating pain. If I were healthy, I would serve Him more. It was easy to put a spiritual face on the desire, but truthfully, I was envious of the health and families God gave others.

As I read Proverbs 27:4, the last part caught my attention. We hear teaching on anger and wrath. We know how destructive anger can be. What about the last part of the verse? "…but who is able to stand before envy?"

We don't deny the first part of the verse because we know it's true. However, we often skip the last portion. After all, doesn't envy only affect me? It doesn't hurt anyone else. "I know it's wrong, but I'm working on it" becomes our excuse.

I don't know if the question in this verse, "…who is able to stand before envy?" is about the envious person or the envied person, but I know both suffer when envy is present. When we allow it into our heart, we are not at peace. Our focus is not on God, our hearts are in turmoil, and we are discontented. When we envy another, we cannot build or keep a genuine, godly relationship with them—because envy is impossible to hide. It comes out in our eyes, tight smiles, murmured comments, cutting humor, silence, and so many other ways.

To diagnose envy in our hearts, we need to be sure we know what it is. Webster defines envy as:

1. Pain, uneasiness, mortification or discontent excited by the sight of another's superiority or success, accompanied with some degree of hatred or malignity, and often or usually with a desire or an effort to depreciate the person, and with pleasure in seeing him depressed. Envy springs from pride, ambition or love, mortified that another has obtained what one has a strong desire to possess.
2. A feeling of discontented or resentful longing aroused by someone else's possessions, qualities, or luck.

The first definition I might skip and say, "That's not me. There's no hatred or malignity in my feelings. I don't want to see them depressed." However, the second definition hit home. I've been there. How thankful I am for God's deliverance from envy and His strength to guard against letting it back in! Who is more miserable than the envious person?

Proverbs 14:30 "A sound heart *is* the life of the flesh: but envy the rottenness of the bones."

That is the best description I've ever heard of envy and what it does to a person. It rots, and we all know that rot weakens and contaminates everything good around it. If you don't think this is true, put one rotten apple in with some good ones and see what happens to the surrounding fruit. Or, let rotten boards stay in your floor. Eventually, as the rot spreads, they will weaken and you will fall through.

It is not enough to diagnose the problem. We must also deal with it. When God finally got through my stubbornness and showed me that what started as grief had become envy, it broke me. The nastiness of it sickened me. I confessed my sin and asked God to help me root it out. Each time I felt that pang of envy at another's blessing, it reminds me to thank God for His goodness and surrender my will to His again.

I wish these lessons were 'one and done' like learning 2+2=4. You understand it, and you move on to something else. I find I am tested repeatedly on the spiritual lessons I learn. I had to die daily, sometimes hourly, in this area. It was hard, but worth it. I cannot describe the blessing of living in joy and peace instead of envy and bitterness.

One reason I found this lesson so difficult is my desire for "fairness". I had a distinct idea of what I thought was fair or unfair from the time I was a small child. Regardless of how many times my parents reminded me that life isn't fair, I would mutter under my breath, "Well, it should be. It's just not right!" It didn't matter if it was me or another who was facing the unfair circumstances. My childish mind struggled to understand how unfair circumstances could be right.

Through the trials God allowed, I realized God was using life's unfairness to mold me and make me into the person He wanted me to be. I started learning how to surrender the illusion of control and accept what God allowed as best for me. I learned to ask Him what He wanted to teach me and how He wanted to change me through it instead of asking, "Why me?"

Having suffered the rotting effects of envy, I don't want anyone else to endure that. Along with the definition of envy, let's look at some symptoms that help determine if we harbor envy in our hearts.

Discontent or resentment at someone else's blessings. Do you struggle with the accomplishments and blessings of others, even when blended with happiness for them, like I did?

Unhealthy competition. Do you always need to be right, first, or best? It's good to work on being the best you can be, but the need to always be first or the best is a red flag that you struggle with envy.

A need for recognition. Do you get angry, frustrated, hurt, or sad when you don't get recognition for what you contribute to your family, work, church, school, or any other area of your life? Envy or pride are at the root of this.

Obsession with social media. I see this often. It is easy to forget that social media only shows us carefully chosen slices of someone's life, and that can lead to envy. Do you obsessively scroll through social media, only to leave it feeling less joyful than you started? Comparison is the thief of joy! Constantly comparing yourself to others can be a sign of envy.

Negativity and gossip. If you most often focus on the negative, it could be because of envy. We should see and share God's blessings, not focus on the negative. When I was filled with envy, I always saw the negative. Remember, what we see as negative may be God positively working in our lives.

Bitterness or resentment. These can stem from envy. If you are harboring envy, it can cause bitterness or resentment. If either of these are present, look for envy, too.

Envy is the opposite of contentment. One thing that helped me was to remember that my life was in the Lord's hands. If I need something, God promises to provide it. That means if He hasn't provided it, I don't need it.

Realizing this helped me trust the Only wise God to give me what I needed, and rest in His plan for me. As I trusted Him and focused on His power and goodness, I traded the rottenness of envy for the peace and joy of trusting Him. The battle isn't easy, but it's always worth it.

Chapter Fourteen

God Always Does Right

Genesis 18:25 "…Shall not the Judge of all the earth do right?"

God always does right. When I was growing up, I often heard my dad speak these words, or minor variations of them. He constantly reminded us (and others) that no matter how hard, disappointing, or unfair circumstances may seem to be, we can always rely on the surety that God will never do wrong. Through the years, these words have steadied and encouraged me when life's storms threatened to overwhelm. I always knew that God was in control and that He would only do what was good.

These words came back to comfort and encourage me in the days after our first miscarriage. My husband and I were all set to announce the wondrous news that God was giving us a child when a routine ultrasound showed all was not well. Within a week, I miscarried. God took our child Home before we could meet them. Our hearts grieved this loss, but our spirits remained strong as we reminded ourselves that God is in control and He always does right.

However, I lost sight of this truth as we endured one miscarriage after another. I still knew the truth, but I lost sight of it as I listened to my feelings and the lies of the enemy. How could this be right? How could others have a houseful of children while we ached with empty arms?

I am thankful that God doesn't give up on us so easily. He patiently brought me back to this truth as many times as it took for me to learn the lesson. I am amazed and blessed when I see God bring back the lessons that I learned in my childhood to encourage me when the real difficulties come. That He patiently teaches me the same lesson repeatedly is even more amazing.

I should have learned this lesson sooner since it is all throughout Scripture. King Saul unfairly hounded David, but God was using it to train David for the job ahead. Out of this unfairness came the most beautiful psalms. It was unfair that Sarah was barren, but God used that to grow her faith. Naomi thought God had treated her unfairly and harshly, yet God used her trials to bring Ruth to Israel so she could be in the lineage of Christ. The most amazing example of all: Jesus Christ, the Son of God, allowed men to treat Him unfairly on His journey to the cross. He did this for us. How can I complain when I face 'unfair' circumstances?

After several years, I realized God was using life's unfairness to mold me and make me into the person He wanted me to be. I started learning how to turn loose of the illusion of control and accept what God allowed as what was best for me. I learned to ask Him what He wanted to teach me and how He wanted to change me through it. This focus shift has allowed me to walk through other unfair situations with much more grace and contentment than I had before. Why? Because I realized and trusted that God always does right. People may not do right. Circumstances may feel or be unfair, but none of that matters. As a child of God, nothing touches me without His permission.

I thank God that my parents faithfully taught me these lessons. Without them, I would sulk and allow bitterness to take over. Instead, I confessed the sin of bitterness and shut the door on it. Each time the temptation comes to focus on the unfair situation, I can instead choose to focus on the truth that God always does right.

As I wrote the first draft of this chapter, we had six days left to get the paperwork in for our visa applications in Brazil. It was our third try. We were working through a lawyer because everything was in Portuguese and we hadn't learned the language. The first time we applied, the Brazilian consulate in the USA lost our paperwork. The second time, our lawyer missed some details, and they denied our application because the paperwork wasn't complete. Then he didn't tell us we had to have certain certifications on our documents. So, we had to mail them home to be certified in three different states. One state refused to do what they said they would on their website. Another failed to use the Priority mailer we sent to return the paperwork, so it took longer for it to arrive. The third state had lost a signature on file, so we had to apply for a new birth certificate and get it certified after they issued it.

We were not the ones who messed things up. It would be easy to focus on how easily others have gotten their visas, or how unfair it was that we suffer because someone else didn't do their job. But truthfully, whether we got to stay or had to go home, it was in God's hands. He is the One who chooses where we go. We wanted to stay and continue working with the people we had learned to love, but God had other plans. The last of our paperwork arrived the day after the deadline and we had to leave Brazil. With sad, but settled, hearts, we packed up and returned home.

Less than one month after we returned home, my dad went to Heaven, and we were with him and my family. The next month, my husband's mother spent some time in ICU and we were home so we could stay with her until she was strong enough to be on her own again. Finally, God directed my husband into a new and unexpected missions project. God had plans for us, and although it looked unfair that we could not get visas, God was working His plan and it was good. I'm so glad we trusted Him.

With those childhood lessons in mind, I can move forward through any storm. My life is in my Heavenly Father's very capable hands. He knows what is best for me, and I know that He always does what is right.

Lilias Trotter, missionary to Algiers, wrote the following in one of her journals during a particularly dark period.

> "January was one of the darkest and toughest months we've ever had. One literally could do nothing but pray at every available moment. Still, the light does not come, just a blind holding on to a dim Christ."

Sometimes, as Lilias Trotter wrote, we cannot see what God is doing, but we can hold on to Him in blind faith, knowing He is working even when we cannot see it. We can also cling to the truth that God will always do right. Lilias, and those working with her, eventually saw light in their work. But they would never have seen the blessings if they had given up because they didn't trust God in the darkest times.

My friend, never give up. The enemy wants your destruction. People, even friends, will fail and disappoint you, but God *always* does right.

---

[7] Miriam Huffman Rockness. 2003. *A Passion for the Impossible : The Life of Lilias Trotter*. Grand Rapids, Mi: Discovery House Publishers. Page 160

Chapter Fifteen

Trust

Proverbs 3:5-6 "Trust in the LORD with all thine heart; and lean not unto thine own understanding. ⁶In all thy ways acknowledge him, and he shall direct thy paths."

We have talked much about trusting God. In grief, we often search for understanding; why did this happen? It is human nature to look for a reason, for someone to blame, or a way to make sense of it. We talked about this in "Purpose in Pain", but what if God doesn't want us to understand? What if He wants us to trust Him without understanding what He is doing?

Verse 5 of Proverbs 3 tells us to trust in the Lord with all our hearts and not to lean on our understanding. I don't have to understand what God is doing. Even if I understand why, it wouldn't give me the peace or strength I need. That comes only from trusting God.

I can testify to this in my life. I know and trust God more than I did before I walked the valleys.

Turning loose of my need to understand and fully trusting God was a huge part of my path to healing and joy. My question turned from "Why?" to "What do you want to teach me? Is there some sin you want to reveal and purge? Is there something you want me to learn? I want to know You more. I want You to use me."

So, if we can't trust our own understanding, what do we do when the bottom drops out of our world and we find ourselves in the darkest part of the valley?

In all thy ways, acknowledge Him

It is easy to see what is wrong with our situation and focus on that. We see what someone else should or should not have done.

In our Brazil visa situation, several people didn't do their job properly. It caused us a lot of trouble and cost us a lot of money. Daily, Satan tempted me to focus on that. "If they had/hadn't…" But truthfully, our situation was never in their hands. It was in God's hands and we are His to do with as He wills. I had to acknowledge Him, His power, and His will. That removes the stress and gives rest.

Be not wise in your own eyes

Seeking God's wisdom is always better than our own. I have a terrible habit of thinking I know what should happen. As someone who struggles with organization, I want to make plans and follow them. To trust God, I have to set aside my ideas and seek His wisdom, resting in Him, especially when my plans go awry.

Fear the Lord

If we fear the Lord, we don't need to fear men. Too often, we fear men in our trials. This is especially tempting when our trial is because someone else made a mistake or sinned against us. Even in this, God doesn't want us to fear them. Our focus should be on Him. The book, *When People are Big and God is Small* by Edward T. Welch, brought home to me how often I am guilty of looking at people as if they are big and this leads to considering God as small in my life. If I fear another person, and it doesn't drive me to the Master for help, I am guilty of thinking that person is bigger and more influential in my life than God. What a terrible way to treat my Creator!

Depart from evil

It is not our place to sort someone else out, but it is our job to make sure we are right with God. We know we cannot hear God if we are harboring sin in our hearts. Keeping short accounts with God, quickly confessing and forsaking sin in our lives, is imperative if we want God to direct us. When we have been going through trials, it is especially important to make sure we are not harboring anger, bitterness, or fear. These are often the biggest temptations.

He shall direct

With our hearts right and attuned to God, He can readily direct us. If we focus on the trial or those responsible, we can miss what God is trying to teach us, or miss His leading. But if we focus on Him, and fear Him instead of man, we can easily hear not only His voice of comfort, but His still small voice directing us.

> Proverbs 3:8 "It shall be health to thy navel, and
> marrow to thy bones."

One of the leading causes of disease in our country is stress. If you search for physical symptoms of stress online, you will find thousands of sites. It destroys our health and it can kill us. Trusting the Lord, however, brings health, according to Proverbs 3:8. I do not say stress causes every illness. That would be foolish. Sometimes it is part of the trial God allows, but when we stress instead of trusting God, we can bring a host of problems on ourselves, sometimes adding to our burden. How much better it is to trust Him, rest in Him, and let Him direct us, and give us peace?

> Isaiah 55:8-9 For my thoughts *are* not your thoughts,
> neither *are* your ways my ways, saith the LORD. [9]For
> *as* the heavens are higher than the earth, so are my

ways higher than your ways, and my thoughts than your thoughts.

If God was small enough to be understood, He wouldn't be big enough to trust. Let us follow the example of the Apostle Paul.

2 Corinthians 4:7-18 "But we have this treasure in earthen vessels, that the excellency of the power may be of God, and not of us. [8]*We are* troubled on every side, yet not distressed; *we are* perplexed, but not in despair; [9]Persecuted, but not forsaken; cast down, but not destroyed; [10]Always bearing about in the body the dying of the Lord Jesus, that the life also of Jesus might be made manifest in our body. [11]For we which live are alway delivered unto death for Jesus' sake, that the life also of Jesus might be made manifest in our mortal flesh. [12]So then death worketh in us, but life in you. [13]We having the same spirit of faith, according as it is written, I believed, and therefore have I spoken; we also believe, and therefore speak; [14]Knowing that he which raised up the Lord Jesus shall raise up us also by Jesus, and shall present *us* with you. [15]For all things *are* for your sakes, that the abundant grace might through the thanksgiving of many redound to the glory of God. [16]For which cause we faint not; but though our outward man perish, yet the inward *man* is renewed day by day. [17]For our light affliction, which is but for a moment, worketh for us a far more exceeding *and* eternal weight of glory; [18]While we look not at the things which are seen, but at the things which are not seen: for the things which are seen *are* temporal; but the things which are not seen *are* eternal."

Chapter Sixteen

King of Kings

Revelation 17:14 "These shall make war with the Lamb, and the Lamb shall overcome them: for he is Lord of lords, and King of kings: and they that are with him *are* called, and chosen, and faithful."

Many people only think of Jesus as the baby in a manger or hanging on the cross. I love to remember that He is King. He is not just any king; He is the King of kings. Every other king in the world's history has been, or will be, defeated. Other kings or enemies overcame some. A few destroyed themselves by their own foolish choices or weak wills. Death ultimately defeated (or will defeat) them all. Jesus is the only king that conquered death.

When we get discouraged during trials, especially ongoing trials, we are usually believing one of two lies: God isn't powerful enough to sort out this mess, or God doesn't care enough. Our enemy tells us these lies to keep us from getting victory.

This is the opposite of what the Bible says about God's power and His love as our King.

Our King's Power

God's power is a significant source of encouragement to me. His reign as the only undefeatable king reminds me of His complete power. Satan has provoked many to attempt to defeat God or thwart God's plan, but none have succeeded. No one ever will.

Sometimes, rulers or other people in our lives appear to be in control, and things seem hopeless. Yet we must remember He can even turn the heart of a king. The power that makes Him undefeatable is the same power that works on my behalf. I must never believe the lie that something is too hard for God. He has absolute power.

> Proverbs 21:1 "The king's heart *is* in the hand of the LORD, *as* the rivers of water: he turneth it whithersoever he will."

Sweet peace comes when I remember God can turn the king's heart in any direction He chooses. This has been a great encouragement and comfort to me when those in power seemed to hold all the control. Those against us may think they are in control, but they're not. They have only such power as God allows them, for as long as He allows.

King Nebuchadnezzar discovered this. He thought he was in control. Daniel warned him against this pride, begging him to humble himself before God. Yet, one day, the king walked out to survey his kingdom and reveled in all "he had created." Immediately, the King of Heaven rebuked him.

> Daniel 4:30-33 "The king spake, and said, Is not this great Babylon, that I have built for the house of the kingdom by the might of my power, and for the honour of my majesty? [31]While the word *was* in the king's mouth, there fell a voice from heaven, *saying,* O king Nebuchadnezzar, to thee it is spoken; The kingdom is departed from thee. [32]And they shall drive thee from men, and thy dwelling *shall be* with the beasts of the

field: they shall make thee to eat grass as oxen, and seven times shall pass over thee, until thou know that the most High ruleth in the kingdom of men, and giveth it to whomsoever he will. [33]The same hour was the thing fulfilled upon Nebuchadnezzar: and he was driven from men, and did eat grass as oxen, and his body was wet with the dew of heaven, till his hairs were grown like eagles' *feathers,* and his nails like birds' *claws.*"

Nebuchadnezzar was undoubtedly powerful. Like many other kings, he considered himself a self-made man. He had wealth, power, and a lot of pride. He thought he was in control, but he was to learn control is an illusion. God is the only one in control.

Because Nebuchadnezzar failed to humble himself when Daniel warned him, God humbled him. Imagine the most powerful king in the known world living like an animal until he blessed, praised, and honored the King of kings. When he did this, God restored him to his throne. God's great power has not weakened. This same power works on our behalf when we trust Him.

Our King's Love

The second lie of Satan is that God doesn't care enough. A God with great power is wonderful, but only if He cares. Many kings and rulers have the power to help their people, but they use their power only to help themselves, allowing those under their care to suffer and die. Other kings have the power to help, but their policies and programs help groups of people. They do not individually touch the lives of every subject.

Our King is different. He knows every person and each specific need, and He personally intervenes in our lives. Life may not go the way we want it to, but we can rest in knowing that the God who knows us best is the same God that promises to meet our needs. We often say, "I need___ (fill in the blank)." But if God hasn't supplied it, we don't need it. We know this because He promised to supply our every need.

Philippians 4:19 "But my God shall supply all your need according to his riches in glory by Christ Jesus."

God also cares about us and our burdens. He is always ready to hear us if we are not regarding iniquity in our heart. (See Psalm 66:18.) With an earthly king, you may or may not get an audience with him. You must request a hearing, give a reason for it, and wait for them to schedule or deny your request. Our King is always available. In fact, He encourages us to come to Him.

Hebrews 4:16 "Let us therefore come boldly unto the throne of grace, that we may obtain mercy, and find grace to help in time of need."

Our King wants us to come boldly before His throne. He wants to hear from us because He loves us. Coming boldly to God isn't arrogance, but confidence that comes from knowing and trusting Him.

My Responsibility

It's lovely to think of a king with the power and the desire to work in my life. Yet I must also look at my responsibility. Having a great king means I am His subject. He rules, I obey. This is the way it is supposed to be. Too often, we want God to show His power, demonstrate His care, and then we want to go on and do our own thing, making choices based on what we want out of life. As the daughter of the King of kings, my responsibility is to live to please Him. This means submitting my will to His. John the Baptist stated it succinctly.

John 3:30 "He must increase, but I *must* decrease."

Christ must have preeminence in my life. His will must be all that matters to me. I must not make life choices based on what I want, but on what He wants. My entire life should be about pleasing and serving my King.

This includes submitting to the valleys He leads me through, trusting that He is working it for good. How can I say I trust God when I complain about the valleys? Submitting to my King means submitting to everything, not just the parts I like. It is impossible to describe how this truth changed my life. I can rest in the most uncertain situations. I can trust Him through the hardest trial. This doesn't make trials easy, but it removes the anxiety. This perfect submission is the only path to peace.

Chapter Seventeen

Perfect Submission

Luke 22:41-42 "And he was withdrawn from them about a stone's cast, and kneeled down, and prayed, [42]Saying, Father, if thou be willing, remove this cup from me: nevertheless not my will, but thine, be done."

I originally wrote the following post while we were on deputation to go to Africa.

> Perfect submission,
> All is at rest.
> I in my Savior am happy and blest.
> Watching and waiting,
> Looking above,
> Filled with His goodness,
> Lost in His love.[8]

---

[8] Crosby, Fanny. 1873. *Blessed Assurance.* http://hymnary.org/text/blessed_assurance_jesus_is_mine.

We sang "Blessed Assurance" at church last night. It is one of my favorite songs, but last night the second and third verses captured my attention most, due to some work that God was doing in my heart.

I sometimes hesitate to write posts like this. They're too transparent for comfort. They show the worst side of me, but they also show the greatness of my God. The hope that my wretchedness and God's greatness may help or encourage someone else urges me onward to write.

This past year has been a mixture of the most wonderful and most difficult six months of my life. On the wonderful side, I am enjoying my new marriage and basking in my husband's love. This man God has given me is truly worth the long wait.[9] Also on the wonderful side are the great churches we have been in and the sweet fellowship we've had with old and new friends on the deputation trail. I'm loving it!

On the most difficult side, is two miscarriages and health problems that keep me exhausted and struggling to get up, get packed, and get moving on this deputation adventure. The exhaustion and physical challenges got worse with each pregnancy and miscarriage. However difficult the physical, it has been nothing compared to the heartache of having two babies see Heaven before I got to see their faces.

After the first miscarriage, I grieved, healed physically, began to heal emotionally, and we had hope that God would give us another child. With the second miscarriage in four months, I couldn't seem to recover as before. I'm not talking about the physical so much as everything else. It seemed everywhere I turned, someone was pregnant, had a new baby, or was

---

[9] I was 42 when we married.

congratulating me on my pregnancy because they hadn't heard of the miscarriage.

Despite all this, I seemed to do fairly well until last weekend. It was Father's Day. The pastor's wife of the church we were in was due to have her baby girl on Monday. I missed my babies. I cried Saturday evening after dinner. I cried all Sunday morning before church and struggled with tears through church. I could hardly make conversation during Saturday's dinner and Sunday lunch and felt guilty for allowing this to consume me and hinder fellowship with this lovely church family. As difficult as it was on me, I grieved because I knew I was making it hard on my husband as well.

Grief is not wrong. However, deep down, I knew that mixed with my grief was anger and the beginning root of bitterness. I tried to ignore that. I tried to call it grief and justify it. After all, I had lost two babies this year. This was natural.

Sunday night I cried through the service again, but these were different tears. God used the evening sermon to finish the work He had started in me during the messages that morning. He faced me with the truth that my anger and bitterness were wrong and had caused most of the agony I had suffered all weekend. I was not rejoicing in the day God had made. I was not accepting His will. Instead, I was clinging to my will and not surrendering it to Him. In my spirit, I was fighting and angry that I didn't get my own way. God gave no wiggle room for me to gloss it over or justify it, even in my own eyes. It was an unsubmissive spirit. It was sin.

This week has been so much better. I am still exhausted and I am still struggling with health issues. I still miss my babies. Despite all this, there is also perfect rest, and I in my Saviour am happy and blessed. It's true. Submission brings rest. Submission to my God, submission to my husband (which comes when I am submitted to God), these bring rest and delight even to a soul that is hurting.

Are we willing to never see our desire this side of heaven? Can we fully trust Him, willing to enter into the fellowship of His suffering?[10]

There have been many more opportunities to practice submission during trials since I wrote this post. Sometimes I succeeded and sometimes I failed to surrender my will to His. I have proved repeatedly that focusing on what I want only brings turmoil, but submission to Him brings rest.

Christ gives us the ultimate example of submission to the Father. Although He speaks often of doing His Father's will, it is in the Garden of Gethsemane that we see it most vividly. Jesus is facing the cross. He knows what awaits Him, so He gets alone with His Father. While praying, He says, "O my Father, if it be possible, let this cup pass from me: nevertheless not as I will, but as thou *wilt*" (Matthew 26:39). He is not facing betrayal, mocking, torture, shame, crucifixion, and separation from the Father for His own wrong. He is facing it all for me. As He faces the horrors to come, He asks for deliverance, then offers His submission.

In July 2015, we were preparing to go to Botswana, Africa. After five miscarriages, I was expecting again. Fear vied with hope. When I started not feeling well, I put myself on bed-rest until I could get in to see someone. I hoped and prayed the progesterone and rest would give us the miracle we longed for, a healthy pregnancy and full-term birth. As the familiar symptoms came, I poured out my heart to the Lord. I wanted this child, and if there was any way, please let me carry this baby safely. "Nevertheless, not my will, but Thine be done." His will was not the same as mine. Two days after my 45th birthday, just

---

[10] Philippians 3:10

six weeks before leaving for the mission field, our last baby joined the others in Heaven.

Like many lessons, "Perfect Submission" is not a once-and-done lesson. It is a daily practice of submitting my will to my Heavenly Father, choosing to trust His perfect plan and find rest in Him.

Chapter Eighteen

Remember God's Great Love

1 John 3:1 "Behold, what manner of love the Father
hath bestowed upon us, that we should be called the
sons of God: therefore the world knoweth us not,
because it knew him not."

In the chapter "Peace in Pain," we talked about meditating on
the right things. The path to peace and grace for our trials is
knowing God and believing the truth. Now I want to look at a
truth that Satan often attacks: Even when it doesn't feel like it,
God loves me.

Remember, even in your pain, God loves you. When the trial
drags on, the grief threatens to overwhelm, strength is almost
gone, the enemy prevails, or the pain incapacitates, it is easy to
listen to the enemy's lies. He loves to cast doubt on God's Word
and character. In fact, he started this in the very beginning with
Eve, "Yea, hath God said...?"

Satan not only questioned God's Word, he questioned God's goodness. When he approached Eve, he laid out the supposed benefits of the forbidden fruit, suggesting that God was withholding good things from them, instead of protecting them. We all know the result of Eve listening to that conversation.

Yet, don't we also listen to his lies or suggestions? "How can God love you and allow such suffering?" "If God is so good and powerful, why doesn't He stop such pain?" "Is this how God rewards you for faithfully serving Him?" These are lies from the enemy and the only way to combat lies is with truth. Where do we find the truth? In the Word of God.

We believe God is love, God loves the world, God loved us enough that Jesus died and took our sin upon Him so that we might have eternal life. We can quote verses about God's love and we sing about it. Yet in the darkest hour of our trials, doubt can creep in if we don't guard against it. How can God really love me and allow this? Why would He give His blessings to others and withhold them from me?

Sometimes we think we've messed up and failed so badly that God can no longer love us. How can He still love me when I've disobeyed, failed, or doubted Him? This is also a lie from the enemy. These lies reject the truth of the Bible. God loves us unconditionally. I want to look at some verses that we can meditate on when these lies come whispering through our minds. If we mediate on truth and choose to believe it, the lies cannot take root and destroy our peace.

But remember, this is a choice. We must choose to mediate on truth, no matter how we feel. Feelings lie. Only truth can change them. Regardless of how exhausted or beaten down we are, we dare not take the path of least resistance and allow our minds to dwell on lies. In fact, we dare not even allow our minds to meditate on the truth of what we have lost. We must meditate on Christ and His truth.

These words that Shakespeare penned are true. Think of God's love for you and your love for God as you read them.

> "...love is not love
> Which alters when it alteration finds,
> Or bends with the remover to remove.
> O no, it is an ever-fixed mark
> That looks on tempests and is never shaken;"*[11]

God's love for me does not alter, but do I allow my love for Him to alter when His will is hard?

Truth to Overcome the Lies

Now let's look at some verses we can meditate on when Satan comes with lies. Remember, even Jesus set the example for us by fighting Satan's lies with Scripture.

> John 3:16 "For God so loved the world, that he gave his only begotten Son, that whosoever believeth in him should not perish, but have everlasting life."

Can there be a greater love than this? No. In fact, in John 15:13, Jesus also said, "Greater love hath no man than this, that a man lay down his life for his friends." Jesus Christ, God the Son, put on flesh, lived in this sinful world, suffered, loved, served, endured betrayal, and became sin that I might have a way to the Father. According to 2 Corinthians 5:21, the perfect, holy, spotless Lamb of God *became* sin for me.

Oh, and He did this even though He knew I would sin, doubt Him, and make a mess of things *after* He redeemed me. I cannot comprehend such love. When my pain and sorrow tempt me to think maybe God's love for me has weakened, I need only to look at Calvary to remember His great love for me.

> Romans 8:35-39 "Who shall separate us from the love of Christ? *shall* tribulation, or distress, or persecution, or famine, or nakedness, or peril, or sword? [36]As it is

---

[11] Shakespeare, William.(1609) "Sonnet 116: Let Me Not to the Marriage of True Minds." Poetry Foundation. Accessed August 26, 2024. https://www.poetryfoundation.org/poems/45106/sonnet-116-let-me-not-to-the-marriage-of-true-minds.

written, For thy sake we are killed all the day long; we are accounted as sheep for the slaughter. [37]Nay, in all these things we are more than conquerors through him that loved us. [38]For I am persuaded, that neither death, nor life, nor angels, nor principalities, nor powers, nor things present, nor things to come, [39]Nor height, nor depth, nor any other creature, shall be able to separate us from the love of God, which is in Christ Jesus our Lord."

No tribulation, distress, trial, person, "nor any other creature" can separate us from the love of God. Meditate on this for a while. The love of God is so powerful and unchanging that nothing can ever separate us from it. You cannot face enough sorrow to separate you from God's love. You cannot mess up enough that God will decide to stop loving you. Your sin will hinder your fellowship with Him, but it will not destroy His love for you.

John 17:23 "I in them, and thou in me, that they may be made perfect in one; and that the world may know that thou hast sent me, **and hast loved them, as thou hast loved me**."

Jesus, in His prayer to the Father, declares He has given us the glory that the Father gave Him and He says the Father loves us as He loves Jesus! He doesn't pray this about the disciples only. We know this because verse 20 says He is praying not only for "these alone, but for them also which shall believe on me through their word;". This includes me. I believed on Jesus through the words of these men recorded in Scripture. God, the Father, loves me *as He loves Jesus*!

"Such love, such wondrous love!
That God should love a sinner such as I,
How wonderful is love like this![12]"

---

[12] Bishop, C. 1929. *Such Love*. Brentwood, TN: Lillenas Publishing Co.

Are you finding it hard to feel the love of God today? Does the pain seem to cry out that God surely can't love if He allows such sorrow or sickness? Spend some time meditating on these verses. Look up other verses that remind you of the truth that God loves you, and He will always love you. If you find some verses that help you, write them down so you have them ready every time Satan tries this lie.

> John 15:13-15 "Greater love hath no man than this, that a man lay down his life for his friends. [14]Ye are my friends, if ye do whatsoever I command you. [15]Henceforth I call you not servants; for the servant knoweth not what his lord doeth: but I have called you friends; for all things that I have heard of my Father I have made known unto you."

Chapter Nineteen

God of All Comforts

2 Corinthians 1:3-5 "Blessed be God, even the Father of our Lord Jesus Christ, the Father of mercies, and the God of all comfort; ⁴Who comforteth us in all our tribulation, that we may be able to comfort them which are in any trouble, by the comfort wherewith we ourselves are comforted of God. ⁵For as the sufferings of Christ abound in us, so our consolation also aboundeth by Christ."

A friend and I once taught a series of lessons to our kindergarten class on the attributes and names of God. We learned God is Faithful, the Bread of Life, Forgiving, Eternal, etc. One lesson we taught is God is our Comforter, and The God of all comfort. We knew life would not always go smoothly for the little ones we were teaching. We wanted to teach them where to go for comfort before they needed it.

When Paul was en route to Rome, they endured a terrible storm because Julius, the centurion, ignored Paul's warning and advice. This was not your run-of-the mill storm. It raged for many days and they had given up all hope of being saved. However, the angel of God stood by Paul in the night, gave comfort and cheer, and promised no one would lose their life. Paul passed that comfort on to his fellow-travelers.

While this was a simple lesson written to teach kindergartners that God is always with them and will always be there to comfort them, it is an important reminder for us, too. We can learn how to navigate our storms by studying Paul's response.

Paul did not rant against the storm. He did not demand to steer the boat or help it land. Nor did he go to all the prisoners and guards, telling them Julius was to blame for their predicament. He just rested in the word of Almighty God and trusted Him to sort it all out. Then he passed that comfort on to those on the ship with him.

It is easy to focus on the storm we are going through instead of focusing on Christ. We have to guard against that. Remember how that turned out for Peter? As long as he had his eyes on Jesus, he walked on water. When he saw the waves were boisterous, he sank. This happens to us, too. If we lose sight of God during our storm, the storm begins to overwhelm and drown us.

When God burdened Amy Carmichael to go to the mission field, she counted the cost and had one lingering concern: how it would affect her loved ones, especially her widowed mother and Mr. Wilson, who had unofficially adopted her. We can learn much from Mrs. Carmichael's reply to her daughter.

She recounted the joy and comfort Amy had been to her. In her sorrow, loneliness, and gladness, God had given her Amy as a companion. Considering how God had loaned her this bright daughter, how could she say no when God called Amy to do His will? She recognized Amy was God's child, to send and use as He pleased.

Instead of focusing on her pain in saying goodbye, she gave thanks that Amy heard His voice, and that God met her own need in His Word. She faced the truth of what it would mean to them all to be separated, but encouraged Amy - and herself - to keep their eyes on Him and trust Him.

One of my favorite parts of this letter is how she wonders how we do not more cheerfully and willingly follow Him, considering His wonderful love for us.

Times were different then. Mrs. Carmichael knew when Amy boarded the ship, she might never see her daughter again. Giving her daughter to foreign missions could mean losing her to sickness or death in a strange land. She looked at this truth and counted the cost, but she did not focus on the loss. Mrs. Carmichael only referenced her loss to show how great God's comfort and grace is. She encouraged Amy, and herself, to keep their eyes on God, confident that no wave would swamp them. She knew the truth of Psalm 23 because she walked with the Shepherd.

Psalm 23:4 "Yea, though I walk through the valley of the shadow of death, I will fear no evil: for thou *art* with me; thy rod and thy staff they comfort me."

Amy remained single and gave her life to rescuing children from the horrors of temple slavery in India after a short time of service in Japan. Years later, she would tell one of 'her children' how she faced the Lord with her fear for the future while she was still in Japan.

Amy was feeling fearful about the future, so she went to a cave to be alone with God. The enemy was tormenting her with pictures of a desperately lonely life if she continued in this path God had set for her. As she poured out her heart to God, He gave her Psalm 34:22.

"The LORD redeemeth the soul of his servants: and none of them that trust in him shall be desolate."

That promise sustained Amy, and she testified God had fulfilled it in her life. Amy learned to lean on God, whether she was leaving her mother, risking her life to rescue a child, or facing a life of loneliness. He was sufficient for everything life would bring. She leaned on this sufficient grace and comfort all the way through, including the last nearly 20 years of her life when she lived in constant pain because of a fall. This fall appeared to be a cruel accident, but God used Amy to pen many books while pain confined her to bed. He not only comforted Amy, He used her to comfort others.

We too must trust Him and take comfort in His presence and His promises, regardless of what we face. I have tried Him and found His comfort sufficient for every trial. If harder things come my way, I can rest in knowing His comfort is enough because I know Him and have learned to trust Him and run to Him for comfort.

> 2 Corinthians 1:3-4 "Blessed be God, even the Father of our Lord Jesus Christ, the Father of mercies, and the God of all comfort; ⁴Who comforteth us in all our tribulation, that we may be able to comfort them which are in any trouble, by the comfort wherewith we ourselves are comforted of God."

Chapter Twenty

Almighty God

1 Timothy 1:17 "Now unto the King eternal, immortal, invisible, the only wise God, *be* honour and glory for ever and ever. Amen."

We often see no way to navigate, endure, or resolve our trials. It is easy to feel helpless and get discouraged, but I want to share some hope with you today. Go read Mark 5. Seriously, go read it. I'll wait. You have to see this chapter. I know you've probably already read it a dozen or a hundred times, but I encourage you to read it again. It was such a blessing to me and I want to share some things that encouraged me.

We know trials come in all shapes and sizes. Some are physical, some are spiritual battles, and sometimes it's death we face. This chapter shows Jesus' power over all three.

In verses 1-16, we see He controls the powers of hell. In case you are reading this on the go and couldn't go read Mark 5 right now, the first 16 verses recount the story of the man possessed by demons in the country of the Gadarenes. He lived among the dead, wandering through the tombs, cutting himself and crying. Many had tried to tame him by chaining him, but he broke the chains. His case appeared hopeless. Then he met Jesus and the demons that enslaved him had no power to stay.

Spiritual Battles

Sometimes, the trials we endure come from intense spiritual warfare. It may take the form of wicked men or women fighting against the work of God, or it may come from an individual attacking us personally. Everything they do seems to cause more devastation, and we are powerless against them. It is easy to see them as the enemy and miss the fact that they are tormented, even as they torment us. If they are unsaved, they face an eternity of torment.

We can also forget that they can only go as far as God allows. When we were serving in Africa, one man in a village became angry because we couldn't give him what he wanted. He argued, accused, and said he wouldn't come back to Bible study because we didn't love like Jesus loved.

This happened while we were gathering paperwork to renew our visas. A few weeks later, someone told us they saw him in town and he said he was going to call Immigration and get our permit applications denied and get us deported. In that region, if a local called with a report of a foreigner mistreating citizens, it was possible to get them deported, regardless of whether their report was true. The folks coming to Bible studies were concerned and asked what we were going to do. Our reply, "Nothing. If God wants us to stay, there is nothing he can do to get us deported. If God allows us to be deported, He is finished with us here."

Weeks passed with no word from him. During that time, we finished gathering our paperwork and applied to renew our visas. One Sunday, someone said they saw him in the village. He'd had a farming accident and cut his leg badly. He couldn't travel further than the clinic to get his wound dressed. By the time he could travel to town, we had our 3-year permits, and he dropped it. This was not the last time someone fought against us, but God kept us there until He finished with us in Africa. This man (among others) was not our enemy. He was being used by our enemy. Yet, God was greater and accomplished His will.

> 1 John 4:4 "Ye are of God, little children, and have overcome them: because greater is he that is in you, than he that is in the world."

Physical Battles

The second part of Mark 5 shows us that God controls sickness. Verses 25-34 tells the story of a woman who had almost lost hope. She had been sick for 12 years and spent all her money on doctors who couldn't help her.

Hearing about Jesus, she came to find Him, intent on at least touching his clothes if she couldn't get His full attention. Maybe she didn't want his attention, or maybe she thought she was beneath His attention or not important enough to interrupt what He was doing. Whatever her reason, she simply reached out in faith to touch His garment.

Regardless of whether she wanted it, she had His full attention. When Jesus asked who touched Him, she fell before Him with fear and trembling. Jesus didn't rebuke her for reaching out to Him. He commended her faith and sent her away, healed of her hopeless disease.

If God wants us whole, He can heal us immediately or use doctors or treatments to accomplish it. Cancer, Lyme Disease, autoimmune disorders, or any other "impossible" illness is not too hard for Him. His will may not be healing, but if it is, He has the power to accomplish it.

Death

Lastly, in verses 35-43, we see Jesus' power over death. Jairus must have been impatient at the delay with the woman Jesus healed, yet encouraged to see God's power in action. They were on their way to his house. His daughter was gravely ill, and he was asking Jesus to heal her.

While Jesus is telling this lady she is healed, a servant comes with the news every parent dreads. His daughter is dead. Can you imagine his despair? What if Jesus hadn't stopped? Would that bit of time have made a difference? Jesus comforts Jairus and they continue on their way.

When they arrive at the house, the mourners are already weeping and wailing. Jesus puts them out of her room despite their contempt at His statement that she is not dead. Yet, when the Way, the Truth, and the Life took her hand and told her to arise, death couldn't hold her.

> Revelation 1:18 "*I am* he that liveth, and was dead; and, behold, I am alive for evermore, Amen; and have the keys of hell and of death."

It is easy to despair when trials threaten to overwhelm us. We grow weak and the enemy whispers that there is no hope. Don't listen to that lying voice. Our God is the God that controls everything, even death and the demons of hell.

Do you remember Job? When Satan wanted to tempt Job, God gave him permission, but He set boundaries. Never forget that. God controls the devils, sickness, and even your death. He also sets limits on your trials. So shut out the lying voices and remember, He loves us enough to put us through the fire and enough to stay with us while we're going through it. If He has given or allowed it, His grace is sufficient for it.

> 2 Corinthians 12:9 "And he said unto me, My grace is sufficient for thee: for my strength is made perfect in weakness. Most gladly therefore will I rather glory in my infirmities, that the power of Christ may rest upon me."

Chapter Twenty-One

Unfailing Love

Romans 8:35-39 "Who shall separate us from the love of Christ? *shall* tribulation, or distress, or persecution, or famine, or nakedness, or peril, or sword? [36]As it is written, For thy sake we are killed all the day long; we are accounted as sheep for the slaughter. [37]Nay, in all these things we are more than conquerors through him that loved us. [38]For I am persuaded, that neither death, nor life, nor angels, nor principalities, nor powers, nor things present, nor things to come, [39]Nor height, nor depth, nor any other creature, shall be able to separate us from the love of God, which is in Christ Jesus our Lord."

As mentioned earlier, when we are going through valleys and hard times, one of the first things Satan tempts us to question is God's love. Humanly speaking, if we love someone and have the power to do what they want or what they need, we'll do it, won't we? So, humanly speaking, or humanistically[13] speaking, if God is all-powerful, and if He loves us, then He will fix things for us. Satan comes and questions God's love or his power.

He suggests God is not good enough, doesn't love us enough, or He's not powerful enough to fix the storm we're going through. Yet, this makes little sense even to human reasoning. Parents who want their children to grow up to be wise, strong, problem-solving adults don't fix all the problems for their children or give them everything they want. Why? Because a child who doesn't listen to instructions needs to feel the consequences of his decisions. An unmotivated child doesn't need his parents to step in and make life easier for them. A child needs to learn to study a situation and make wise choices to learn problem solving, not have Dad and Mom do everything for them. They need to be encouraged to work hard and reap the rewards of their efforts.

Often parents must let their children suffer the discomfort of medicine, surgery, therapy, or other medical intervention because it's best for their children. When my brother was little, my parents had to leave his legs in braces to correct a problem with his bones. If Mom had decided it was too cruel to make him suffer wearing those horrid braces, she would have caused him even more pain and trouble when his legs grew more crooked. Her love for him caused her to put him in those braces and leave him there, even if he hated them.

We sometimes believe if God is big enough to fix anything, He should fix everything. We think "He should get me out of this mess I'm in. He should have stopped this grief from ever happening. He should have stopped that person from betraying me. He should have healed me or never let me (or my loved one) get sick or He could have fixed it. Why didn't He?"

If we want to grow in faith and spiritual maturity, we need to endure hardness. If we want to be more like Christ, we'll need to suffer like Christ. We must be careful when we're in the

---

[13] Focused on humans instead of God

middle of a storm not to ask God, "Where are You? Why are You doing this to me?" Instead, try asking, "What do You want me to learn? What do You want to accomplish?" There's a tremendous difference between the two sets of questions. The first focuses on self as it asks, "Why didn't God do what I wanted Him to?" The second focuses on God and His will as it asks, "What do You want out of this? What do You want from me? What do You want me to learn?"

God loved His Son. The Father and the Son were in perfect harmony. Jesus was the perfect, obedient Son. Yet God allowed Jesus Christ to go to the cross and die in my place. If we go by the humanistic reasoning that we use when we ask why God allows us to suffer, we would have to say God didn't love Jesus because He let Him suffer. Of course, we know that's not true. He did it for a purpose. It was love for you and me that sent Jesus to the cross and that caused the Father to allow Him to go to the cross. Love caused God the Father to turn His back on His Son when Jesus became sin for us.

> 2 Corinthians 5:21 "For he hath made him to *be* sin for us, who knew no sin; that we might be made the righteousness of God in him."

God never wastes the experience of his children. We may waste them, but God doesn't. God never says, "Oops, I messed up on that one." God doesn't randomly give His children hard things to endure because He's bored that day or wants entertainment. God gives us what He wants us to go through because He has a purpose and it's always for good.[14]

I know we've talked about this before, but it's imperative that we grasp this, believe it, and cling to it. If we don't, we will always wonder and question. God is always good and God loves us with an everlasting and unconditional love. Our sin can bring consequences and God's correction into our lives, but God doesn't beat us because He's mad at us. As His children, His correction is *always* for our good. So, when the enemy comes

---

[14] Romans 8:28

whispering in your ear that God must not love you because He's allowing you to go through great trials, remember God's great trials always come for a purpose, and it's always a good purpose.

When Hannah was suffering the cruel mocking of her enemy and the reproach of being a barren woman, she couldn't see why God would do this to her. Yet, she cried out to Him, and in his goodness, He gave her the son that she begged for. He didn't give her this son the first time she asked. The answer to her heart's desire was a long time coming. In fact, it didn't come until Hannah came to the place where she said, Lord, if you give me a son, I will give him back to You. Perhaps Hannah had to come to the place where she would willingly give her son because God has a special purpose for him, and that purpose included him being raised in the tabernacle and taught the things of God.

What if Hannah had children without ever coming to the place where she could give up her son? Would there have been a Prophet Samuel? I don't think so. His upbringing would have been much different if she had raised him at home with his family. But God had a purpose for Samuel, so He set out to do something great, even though it caused Hannah pain for a while. Hannah's story has encouraged many people through the years to ask God for impossible things.

Jesus' birth was a different scenario. The angel came to Mary and told her she would give birth to the Messiah. God chose her to carry the Son of God. This was an incredible honor for her, but along with the honor came the cruel dishonor she would endure. Besides Joseph and Elizabeth, we have no record of anyone else close to them believing this was a virgin birth. Joseph didn't even believe her until the angel told him it was true. She lived with the shame of being considered an adulterous woman. Even though she was not guilty, she and Joseph had to live with that stigma, and so did their children. And yet, this shame, reproach, and sorrow that came into her life was also the source of great joy over being chosen to bear and raise the Son of God. It was God's plan, and He had a purpose for it. Yes, Mary suffered, but it was not random suffering. It was because God had a purpose and a plan.

Please embrace this truth. God allows suffering in your life for a purpose. This suffering He allows is because He has a plan for you. He has something mighty He wants to do. If we will submit to it, we will see God do great things and we'll look back in victory and praise, just like Hannah and Mary.

However, if we don't submit and trust Him, if we endure our suffering with bitterness or self-focus, we will miss the goodness and the blessings of God. Or we'll see them at the end of our trial as we look back with regret and heartache because we didn't trust Him.

When the enemy suggests God loves someone else more because of their blessings, remember God's love does not change based on our circumstances. God's love is not stronger for some than it is for others. He died for all of us. He gave His life for me, and He gave His life for you. In John 15:13, Jesus told His disciples, "Greater love hath no man than this, that a man lay down his life for his friends." Then He turned around and gave his life for us. No greater love. This unconditional, unfailing love is ours, and no one can ever take it away from us.

This truth can be especially hard to learn for someone who grew up in a performance-based acceptance home or church. Performance-based acceptance says if you don't measure up, you're not accepted. This isn't what God says.

Ephesians 1:6-7 "To the praise of the glory of his grace, wherein he hath made us accepted in the beloved. 7In whom we have redemption through his blood, the forgiveness of sins, according to the riches of his grace;"

My acceptance is based on God's goodness and the riches of His grace. If it were based on my performance, I would never be accepted. I'm so thankful for God's unconditional love. There is nothing I can do to make Him love me more or less than He does right now. Let's look one more time at part of our opening verses.

Romans 8:38-39 "For I am persuaded, that neither death, nor life, nor angels, nor principalities, nor powers, nor things present, nor things to come, [39]Nor height, nor depth, nor any other creature, shall be able to separate us from the love of God, which is in Christ Jesus our Lord."

When you don't feel God's love, when you don't see His plan or understand His purpose in your suffering, trust Him. Trust His Word and His promise that He loves you with an everlasting love.

Chapter Twenty-Two

Brokenness

Psalm 34:18 "The LORD *is* nigh unto them that are of a broken heart; and saveth such as be of a contrite spirit."

As a young, single missionary, I wrote in my prayer letter about a trip we planned to take to a neighboring country:

Oh, how I'm praying that I'll return home changed! I'm asking God to renew and increase my burden and vision for souls on this trip. May God break my heart so I'll never be the same.

Someone from back home emailed this in response to that letter:

A lesson I learned a long time ago is to be careful what you ask for, because you may get it...I got what I wanted, but I didn't want what I got!

My reply:

I am well aware of the lesson you're talking about. Not only have I seen others have their prayers answered, but I've also had some of my prayers answered in ways I never dreamed—or would have wanted. When I prayed/wrote it, I was aware that it was a prayer that could take any turn. To be broken usually means intense pain, whether physical, mental, or emotional. I am not a sadist, and pain is not the lot I'd choose for me, but if that's what it takes for God to do a great work in me, then I'll trust Him through it. I agree with Amy Carmichael:

"To me, there is no more tragic sight than the average missionary. A Hindu bowing down to his idol leaves me unmoved beside it. We have given so much, yet not the one thing that counts; we aspire so high, and fall so low; we suffer so much, but so seldom with Christ; we have done so much, and so little will remain; we have known Christ in part, and have so effectively barricaded our hearts against His mighty love, which surely He must yearn to give His disciples above all people…it is fatally easy to live easily."[15]

God, deliver me from indifference or mediocrity!

When I wrote this, there was one thing in my life that I hoped God wouldn't use for this breaking, yet I offered it to Him too, although I still held it close to my heart. Yes, this was the very thing He used in this part of my journey of brokenness. It was crushing, confusing, and took a long time to heal. Yet, looking back, I see God's hand of mercy and goodness in it. I am grateful that He answered my prayer.

You see, I really wanted God to use me. I had many dreams and desires, but to be used was the constant desire. Yet, I had no idea how unusable I was. Oh, I had computer skills and could

---

[15] Carmichael, Amy. (1932) 2002. *Gold Cord.* Kindle. Fort Washington, PA: CLC Publications.

prepare tracts, Bibles, and other literature to be printed, but I had some serious flaws that hindered me from being used as God wanted to use me.

Many years later, God would use other means to break me and make me more like Him. Each time I learned to hold my dreams more loosely until I could hold each one up to Him with a completely open hand and ask Him to give or take at His pleasure. When God takes one now, there is disappointment and even pain, but there is not that ripping, searing pain that comes when He has to pry the offering out of my clenched hand.

In one of these seasons, it seemed everything I picked up to read touched on the subject of brokenness. Everywhere I read in the Bible, God was breaking someone. This sounds cruel, but God doesn't break His children to destroy them, only to refine and make them more usable.

God removed Abraham from his home and family and delayed giving him the son He had promised until they lost all hope. When God finally gave them Isaac, He asked Abraham to sacrifice Isaac. Through all the trials, failures, and disappointments, we see God make Abraham into a great man and use him to begin the nation that would give us the Savior of the world.

God broke Paul often, only to make him a great missionary and use him to reach the world for Christ. The words he penned as he suffered have strengthened and encouraged countless Christians throughout the ages.

Moses was in the desert for 40 years after fleeing Egypt, and God made him a mighty leader, and the meekest man that ever lived.

Sometimes our breaking comes from our own failings & sin, but the blessings that come from it when we submit to Him are life-changing. Peter was a rough fisherman, impulsive and often out of sync with Jesus, but he was still part of that "inner circle" that was always with Jesus. Then Judas betrayed Jesus and Peter denied even knowing Him. Shame and sorrow flooded him when that rooster crowed and Jesus looked at him.[16]

---

[16] Luke 22:60-62

Peter nearly left the ministry, but Jesus sought him out and restored this broken man. Yet, Peter wasn't the same. The Peter who preached with power on Pentecost and the man who wrote the epistles by his name was a man filled with the power of God. What made such a drastic change? His failure broke him and God used it to change him.

The times of breaking in my life have taken various forms throughout the years: shattered dreams, betrayals, loss, sickness, and more. Your breaking may look different from mine, but the goal is always the same: to make us more like Christ, and to bring Him glory.

If you are reading this book, there's a good chance you are going through a time of breaking. I want to encourage you to rejoice in it. I know that sounds crazy and impossible, but it's not. If this breaking is from the Lord, it means He is still working to make you like Him. If it is from the enemy, it means you are being used by God, and Satan is fighting or God allowed him to afflict you for a reason. Regardless of the source or reason, God can use it to change, refine, grow, and use you.

Are you willing to be broken, to be made into the image of God, to be used for His glory? It has truthfully been said, "Whom God greatly uses, He greatly bruises."

Chapter Twenty-Three

Lily of the Valleys

Song of Solomon 2:1 "I *am* the rose of Sharon, *and* the lily of the valleys."

Cagayan de Oro, Philippine Islands, 1999

I loved the work I was doing, and I loved living with, and learning from, the missionary friends who hosted me. Language lessons were hard, but fun. Life was good, but there was one "fly in the ointment". I was in constant pain, a *lot* of pain. Sometimes, I thought I would lose my mind from it.

I had been in a few car wrecks over the years, and now I was getting intensive chiropractic treatments to correct my increasingly crooked spine. The chiropractor told me it would normally take a few years to fix, but we didn't have that long in the Philippines. He said if I could stand the pain, he could fix it in the year we would be there. So, I agreed and started treatments. I had no idea how much pain was in store.

Part way through these treatments, I was rethinking this decision and questioning the wisdom of it. I was in a fog of pain and felt useless. I was only getting in a couple of hours typesetting each day (I think—it's all a bit of a fog, even today). One day I was typesetting, and the pain was so bad that I asked the Lord why He even had me there. Surely someone else could accomplish so much more. It thrilled me to be used, but I didn't understand why He had me there.

As I was praying, the oscillating fan swung back around toward me and ruffled the pages of my open Bible again. This time, instead of just fluttering and settling back down, a few pages turned, and I glanced over. There at the top of the page, I read Song of Solomon 2:1 and noticed something I had never seen before. The last word was plural, not singular. Valleys, not valley.

God used that verse to encourage me that day. He has often been called the Lily of the Valley. We talk about the Lily of the Valley and sing about the Lily of the Valley. That day He showed me He is the Lily of the valleys. All of them. Not just one valley. Not just a generic lily of a generic valley. He is the Lily of the valleys, every single one of them.

No matter what valley I'm walking through, He is there to perfume the air, gladden the eye, bless the heart, and encourage the spirit. He is the Lily of all our valleys.

I bowed my head and thanked my God for walking every valley with me. With my heart encouraged, I turned back to work another hour with a smile on my face and a song in my heart. I was still in pain, but not discouraged. I have been through many more valleys since that day, and the Lily of my valleys has never failed to meet me there.

> Lamentations 3:21-24 "This I recall to my mind, therefore have I hope. [22]*It is of* the LORD'S mercies that we are not consumed, because his compassions fail not. [23]*They are* new every morning: great *is* thy faithfulness. [24]The LORD *is* my portion, saith my soul; therefore will I hope in him."

One of my greatest fears is that these valleys I walk will be in vain. As the Apostle Paul put it in Galatians 2:2, "lest by any means I should run, or had run, in vain." God has a reason and purpose for the valleys he walks me through. I also know that I have a choice and free will. Will I learn or will I resist? I can draw nigh to Him in love and faith, or I can pull away in anger, hurt, or distrust. It is my choice.

I fear this terrible thing because I lost count of how many times I repeated the same lessons. Too often, I saw a glorious truth, realized Christ's overwhelming love, or remembered God's almighty power, only to forget and find myself back in the same habits as before. I would catch myself looking at others and their blessings instead of looking at Christ and recognizing all He has done for me. When this happens, I must choose to change my focus and rejoice. The flesh is good at allowing seeds of bitterness to grow again. It excels at envying instead of rejoicing.

I wondered how God could keep on loving, teaching, leading, and putting up with my unfaithfulness. Then I read verses like Lamentations 3:21-24 and John 21:15-19. In John, we find Jesus coming to His disciples after His resurrection. Peter had denied Christ and now he had returned to his old life of fishing. Yet, Jesus came looking for him again. Looking at Peter's time with Jesus, I see glimpses of myself. He was impetuous, said foolish things, got in the way, rebuked Jesus, forsook Him, and walked away from the ministry God called him to. Yet, Peter's story doesn't end there because Jesus restored him, refined him, and used him. On Pentecost, Peter stood and preached with power. Throughout Acts, we see God mightily using him, then we read Peter's powerful epistles. God, in His infinite wisdom, saw what Peter would become, not what he was when Jesus called him. He didn't give up, and Peter became a great man of God.

He keeps on because of His mercies, His faithfulness, His compassion. He continues because He loves me. His faithfulness is based on His character, not on my actions. I am so glad

He is faithful. Don't give up in the middle of your valley. Draw close to the Lily of the valleys and trust Him to work through the pain you're enduring. He is faithful to walk with you through every valley.

Chapter Twenty-Four

Be Content

Philippians 4:11 "Not that I speak in respect of want: for I have learned, in whatsoever state I am, *therewith* to be content."

I used to teach a kindergarten class at church. With children ages 4 and 5, there were often tears, whines, and sighs when they didn't get what they wanted. They didn't want *that* for a snack. Someone else got the toy they wanted, or they didn't want the color crayon we gave them or the song we chose. We cheerfully reminded them, "You get what you get, and you don't throw a fit. Be thankful." We were doing our best to teach them to be content. Be thankful for what you receive. Gratitude.

As an adult, I often had to go back and remind myself of this lesson. It is so easy to get discouraged and out of sorts when we don't get what we wanted. When my sister-in-law married my brother at 18, and gave birth to their first child at 19, I was upset that God gave her what I wanted before He gave it to me. (Yes,

I was still that childish at 21.) Why did God give her my dream and leave me wondering what He was doing in my life?

Of course, God didn't leave me wondering forever. Before long, I was helping missionaries and learning different jobs related to publishing the Word of God. I loved it and wouldn't change that experience for anything. When I was 41, God changed my life again and brought my husband into it. After a year of long-distance courtship, we married and began deputation for Africa. While on deputation, I had my 6 miscarriages. This series of miscarriages and multiple health problems prolonged our deputation and delayed our departure for Botswana. It also brought back the temptation to be discontent.

As I kept up with friends and family on social media and we traveled to churches, I often saw pregnancy announcements, birth announcements, and all the other milestones that come with having children. The temptation was always there to grieve because God has given them what He has denied me. I didn't get what I wanted. They got what I wanted. It was like I had reverted to my childhood, spiritually speaking.

When I was growing up, I wanted to marry a preacher and have 6-12 children. I also wanted to be like my mother and grandmothers. They were strong, hard-working ladies. Most of all, I wanted to be godly. I wanted to be a praying lady like my mother and grandmother. As I began miscarrying babies, I lost sight of those most important dreams. Instead, I focused on the dream of motherhood that was slipping through my fingers.

The years of undiagnosed and untreated Lyme Disease and several co-infections caused autoimmune issues. Multiple miscarriages made them worse. This was something else to tempt me to be discontent. How could I be effective on the mission field when I could barely function? I "needed" good health. God patiently taught me that if I needed good health, He would give it to me. Constant pain and fatigue were an opportunity to trust God and learn to be content.

The Apostle Paul wrote in Philippians 4:11, "Not that I speak in respect of want: for I have learned, in whatsoever state I am, *therewith* to be content." Paul did not have all he wanted. He had been persecuted, imprisoned, beaten, mistreated, and suffered deprivation. Yet he had learned to be content.

> Hebrews 13:5 "*Let your* conversation *be* without covetousness; *and be* content with such things as ye have: for he hath said, I will never leave thee, nor forsake thee."

This verse is a straightforward command to be content. We are to be without covetousness and be content with what we have. If I don't have children, I am to be content. If I am thousands of miles away from family, I am to be content. When God chooses not to give me good health, I must be content. This is not if I feel like it or think it is fair. It is not optional. It is a command from my King.

There were many other opportunities to learn contentment through the years. I learned to be content in the Lord when someone betrayed me, lied about me, and sent me hate mail. I learned to be content during covid lockdown, unable to go back to Botswana or on to another field. God taught me contentment again when we had to stay on the field while waiting for our visas to process while Dad's health deteriorated. When we could not get permits to stay in Brazil and we had to return home, I was content. During the uncertain time of seeking God's will for direction in ministry after Brazil, we were content with whatever God told us to do. When we lost support because God changed our ministry, we could be content and rest in God's promise to provide.

My husband and I booked a getaway for our anniversary and to finish writing our books. As we drove from my mom's to our retreat, I read the first draft of the chapters I had written for this book, marking edits so I could begin my rewrite first thing Tuesday morning. We arrived Monday afternoon, settled into the cute Airbnb, and got everything set up so we could start writing the next morning.

Weather shifts, especially from warm to cold, cause my autoimmune symptoms to flare, so it did not surprise me to wake

Tuesday morning with a migraine. It wasn't one of the worst I've ever had. I could still function moderately. I worked on the edits a little, but mostly rested, trying to recover so I could be more productive the rest of the week. Tuesday evening, I felt a familiar pain in my right eye. I have had this before, and it usually leaves me with some cloudy spots in my vision for several days or weeks. The beginning of a writing retreat didn't seem like the best timing for this vision problem to reappear, so I prayed and left it in God's hands.

Unexpectedly, I didn't have cloudy spots, but I got some serious visual distortion. Straight lines dipped in the middle and letters in these wavy sentences looked clipped or distorted. I expected this to clear up like the cloudy issues, but it didn't. By Friday morning, it was worse. In fact, it was bad enough for me to call my eye doctor in North Dakota. They recommended seeing someone locally if it didn't clear up. Since it was worse, instead of better, we checked to see if someone nearby could work me in. One internet search and a phone call later, I had an appointment to see a local doctor.

I was expecting to hear much of the same thing I heard before, but his news was not encouraging. This was something different than before, and there was nothing he could do for it. He does not expect it to get better. It will probably get worse and could eventually cause the loss of the central vision in my right eye.

I am at the beginning of my writing journey, with more books on my mind and in my heart. That means a lot more time at the computer or writing in notebooks. So far, this issue has caused eye fatigue and extra headaches, indicating this could be a harder journey than I expected. Sitting in the chair in the exam room, I had a choice. I could praise God or give in to the discouragement that swept over me. While the doctor made notes and printed the images for me to take back to my own eye doctor, I closed my eyes and surrendered it all to the Lord again.

I refuse to focus on the added difficulty and probable increase in headaches. I *will* praise God for this, too. He is in control and nothing touches me without His permission. I am not excited about the possibility of my vision getting worse, but I am excited to see how God uses this new challenge.

This is what Dr. Terry Coomer, a Biblical counselor, calls "the point of impact.[17]" When life hits us, we have a choice. How will we respond? Will we surrender it to God and thank Him for what He is doing, or will we fall apart and start stressing or get angry? We have no control over what happens to us in so many situations, but we do decide our reactions. We can respond well, surrender to God, trust and praise Him, or we can react in the flesh.

Don't expect this to be easy, especially if you have a habit of giving in to the flesh. Our flesh does not like to be crucified, and it fights us. But I am here to share with you from personal experience that living in the flesh may be the path of least resistance, but it is no way to live. It brings discontent, frustration, anger, stress, depression, and all the ugly things we want to escape. Crucifying the flesh and surrendering to God, choosing to praise and thank Him for every circumstance, is the path to peace, joy, contentment, and all the other blessings we long for.

It doesn't matter if it's death, betrayal, foolish people who make your life harder, ill health, natural disasters, loneliness, abuse, or anything else life can throw at us. I have found that when I surrender "at the point of impact" and choose to trust and praise God, His peace supersedes any pain the circumstances may cause.

I am sitting at my computer with my eye aching and tired, the lines of text waving and distorting. Occasionally, I have to close my right eye to see something well enough to fix it. I can focus on the pain and inconvenience and ask "why me and why now?", or I can continue to trust God to use my writing and praise Him anyway. I choose to praise. And with that praise and thanksgiving comes a peace that conquers the lifelong dread of possibly losing my sight, even in one eye.

---

[17] Coomer, Dr. Terry. 2023. *How to Have a Real Relationship with God.* Great Falls, MT: Hope Biblical Counseling and Training Center.

What are you facing today? Has life impacted you, tempting you to give in to anger, fear, despair, or frustration? I challenge you, I even dare you, to put God to the test. Surrender it all to Him and praise Him for it now. Thank Him for it, and for what He is going to accomplish through it. Sing some praises, and wait to see what God will do. I promise, He is able, and He is worthy of our praise, even when life overwhelms.

How did I make this journey from a discontented child to contentment? I learned to remind myself daily that God is in control. He promises to meet my needs, so if He has not provided it, I don't need it. I may want it, but I don't need it, or I don't need it yet. Remember this verse?

Isaiah 26:3 "Thou wilt keep *him* in perfect peace,
whose mind *is* stayed *on thee:* because he trusteth in thee."

This lesson harks back to the lessons we've looked at about how to focus our minds. If we keep God as our focus, we will be content. If we focus on what we want, or don't want, we will struggle with discontentment. The choice is ours.

Chapter Twenty-Five

Be Still

Psalm 46:1-11 "God *is* our refuge and strength, a very present help in trouble. [2]Therefore will not we fear, though the earth be removed, and though the mountains be carried into the midst of the sea; [3]*Though* the waters thereof roar *and* be troubled, *though* the mountains shake with the swelling thereof. Selah. [4]*There is* a river, the streams whereof shall make glad the city of God, the holy *place* of the tabernacles of the most High. [5]God *is* in the midst of her; she shall not be moved: God shall help her, *and that* right early. [6]The heathen raged, the kingdoms were moved: he uttered his voice, the earth melted. [7]The LORD of hosts *is* with us; the God of Jacob *is* our refuge. Selah. [8]Come, behold the works of the LORD, what desolations he hath made in the earth. [9]He maketh wars to cease unto the end of the earth; he breaketh the bow, and cutteth the spear in sunder; he burneth the chariot in the fire. [10]Be still, and know that I *am* God: I will be exalted among the heathen, I will be exalted in the earth. ¹¹The LORD of hosts *is* with us; the God of Jacob *is* our refuge. Selah."

We are all familiar with verse 10 of this chapter: "Be still, and know that I am God." Today, I often see the first part of verse 5 quoted out of context (The "her" in verse 5 is a city, not a person.) I seldom see either used with their context, but using verse 10 alone weakens the message. The context is a powerful reminder that God is our refuge and help, and a reminder of His great power, even in desperate circumstances.

I love the simple, yet profound, opening statement of this psalm. "God *is* our refuge and strength, a very present help in trouble." I cannot imagine anything more comforting and calming in the middle of life's trials than this. The God of Heaven is my refuge, strength, and help. Not just any kind of help, a very present help. He is never missing when we need Him. His strength is perfect, always enough. There is no refuge I would rather have.

> "Therefore will not we fear, though the earth be removed, and though the mountains be carried into the midst of the sea; ³*Though* the waters thereof roar *and* be troubled, *though* the mountains shake with the swelling thereof. Selah."

Because of His perfect strength and help, I have no reason to fear. Every tendency to fear should only drive me to the refuge of my Saviour. I consider the imagery of these verses. Having been in earthquakes and on rough seas, I know how scary it can be. None of this should cause us to fear.

I once read a story about a little girl who sat in her airplane seat, calmly reading, while the other passengers panicked during a turbulent storm. After they landed, someone asked her why she didn't get scared during the storm. She replied she wasn't afraid because her daddy was the pilot.

We can have that same child-like confidence in the middle of our storms, whatever shape they take. In grief, He promised to be our comfort. Has someone betrayed you? Jesus suffered betrayal too, and He is your very present help. Poor health plaguing you and keeping you weak? He, the Great Physician, knows and can heal or give grace according to His plan. Are you in a battle through no fault of your own? He knows and is there with you to fight for you. Are you in trouble because of your own decisions? Read (or reread) the chapter titled, "All Things." He is all you need, regardless of the cause of your trouble.

> "*There is* a river, the streams whereof shall make glad
> the city of God, the holy *place* of the tabernacles of the
> most High. [5]God *is* in the midst of her; she shall not be
> moved: God shall help her, *and that* right early. [6]The
> heathen raged, the kingdoms were moved: he uttered
> his voice, the earth melted. [7]The LORD of hosts *is* with
> us; the God of Jacob *is* our refuge. Selah."

Oh, the riches we find in these verses! Did you notice verse 6? I know many who are enduring trials because wicked people are causing trouble with their lies. The heathen often rage, seeking to destroy others in their misery. Sometimes their attempts to destroy take the shape of false accusations. In some places, the wicked kill Christians for their faith. Do not despair, my friend. Our God is so powerful that His voice can melt the earth. Stop and consider this for a moment. He doesn't have to move, only speak. He may allow you to be in the fire for a time, but He is more powerful than anyone or anything. When He says the trial is over, it will end. Your enemies are not in control. God is.

While it seems unbearable to go through the trials that come our way, never forget that through it all, the Lord of hosts is with us. The God of Jacob is our refuge. Go back and read some of the powerful miracles God did, then remember His power has not diminished.

> "Come, behold the works of the LORD, what
> desolations he hath made in the earth. [9]He maketh wars
> to cease unto the end of the earth; he breaketh the bow,

and cutteth the spear in sunder; he burneth the chariot in the fire."

Looking back at God's greatness, and remembering His miracles, can encourage us to trust Him. Come, behold the works of the LORD: look and remember His power. When we do this, it helps us follow the directive in our favorite verse. "Be still, and know that I *am* God." The last part of our favorite verse is a declaration that God will be exalted. This is not a hope, or a perchance. He *will* be exalted.

"The LORD of hosts *is* with us; the God of Jacob *is* our refuge. Selah."

This last verse reminds us He is with us, our refuge. Too often we break in the middle of trials, overwhelmed with the storm. Our hearts fail. We get fearful, frustrated, angry, bitter, anxious, and stressed. This happens when we focus on the storm. What if we focused on the LORD of hosts instead?

In Genesis 39, when Joseph told the chief butler what his dream meant and asked him to speak to Pharaoh on his behalf, I believe Joseph realized God had sent the butler there for Joseph's deliverance. Imagine how easily Joseph could have become discouraged when two years went by before he was released from that prison. Sometimes we are right about what God is doing, but wrong about the timing. Don't get discouraged when God doesn't work when you expect Him to. Be still and trust Him.

Chapter Twenty-Six

What is That to Thee?

John 21:20-22 "Then Peter, turning about, seeth the disciple whom Jesus loved following; which also leaned on his breast at supper, and said, Lord, which is he that betrayeth thee? ²¹Peter seeing him saith to Jesus, Lord, and what *shall* this man *do?* ²²Jesus saith unto him, If I will that he tarry till I come, what *is that* to thee? follow thou me."

I find this one of the most intriguing passages in Scripture. In chapter 20, Jesus showed Himself to the disciples, including "doubting" Thomas. Chapter 21 opened with Peter going back to fishing and taking the others with him. Christ revealed Himself to them after a fruitless night of fishing, filled their nets, and served them a fish dinner.

Next, we read those three famous "Lovest thou me" questions and answers. After telling Peter to feed His sheep, Christ alludes to how Peter will finish his life: imprisoned and dying for Christ's sake.

> John 21:18-19 "Verily, verily, I say unto thee, When thou wast young, thou girdedst thyself, and walkedst whither thou wouldest: but when thou shalt be old, thou shalt stretch forth thy hands, and another shall gird thee, and carry thee whither thou wouldest not. [19]This spake he, signifying by what death he should glorify God. And when he had spoken this, he saith unto him, Follow me."

Jesus just restored Peter after his denial and return to his old life. Then Jesus told him that he will live to be old, he will be imprisoned, and he will die a martyr's death. This revelation could bring up a host of questions or thoughts. One would think these most recent words of Christ would consume his thoughts, and maybe he would have questions about the specifics.

However, Peter does an interesting thing. He looks around, sees John, and asks Jesus, "Lord, and what shall this man do?" It is a strange question with peculiar timing. Jesus just gave him a unique glimpse into his life and his death, yet he's asking for a glimpse into someone else's life.

To me, the question seems out of place and unusual until I look around. I see the same thing today. I even catch myself doing it. When facing a valley, we look around to see how others are faring. We ask God, "What about them?"

I read an article somewhere online that mentioned this tendency in dealing with infertility. It started me thinking about this question and Christ's answer. In trials, we often look around and see others who seem to flourish. They don't appear to have the troubles and heartaches we are facing. We ask God, "Why do they get this blessing, but I don't?" Or we ask, "Why do I have to endure such trials, but they seem to thrive without suffering?" "Why do they see the blessings, but I can barely see through the tears?" I've heard so many variations of these questions through the years and even asked some of them myself.

I've watched this play out with single ladies who reach their late 20s, 30s, or 40s. They begin to wonder why every 18-year-old girl in church is getting married, but they're still single and alone. What is wrong with her? The enemy whispers and shouts at her by turns. "You're too strict." That's his temptation to get her to loosen her standards. When that doesn't work, he throws lie after lie at her. She knows he's a liar, but sometimes it's hard to hold to truth when she's bombarded with lies. She loves celebrating with her friends, but it's getting harder and harder to keep a smile on her face while her heart breaks inside. Will it ever be her turn? Something must be wrong with her or God must be angry with her. She wishes she knew which one. It is getting harder to keep her eyes on God and not on everyone else who seems to get the blessing she most longs for.

I've seen the same focus in some families who weep over wayward children, with some couples who cannot have children, or when sickness and death come.

I love Jesus' reply to this question. It brings everything back into focus and balance. What is that to thee? Follow thou me.

Peter, is it your business what I do in another man's life? You follow me. He should not get distracted by what God did or didn't do in John's life. Peter's sole responsibility was to keep his eyes and focus on Christ and follow Him.

The same is true for us. We should not get distracted by what God is doing in someone else's life. Their blessings and sorrows are from the Father, for them alone. Our blessings and trials are from the Father for us alone.

When we compare ourselves with another, either pride or discontent usually follows. 2 Corinthians 10:12 tells us, "...they measuring themselves by themselves, and comparing themselves among themselves, are not wise." This is an important principle. The key to lasting peace and joy is keeping our eyes on Christ and trusting His plan for us as we follow Him. Seek Him.

Scripture shows us God deals with individuals differently. Even Jesus' miracles illustrate this truth. For some miracles, He simply spoke. At other times, He touched those He healed.

Once, Jesus spit in the dirt and made mud to put on a blind man's eyes. Then He told him to go wash his eyes. What if that man had complained because Jesus used a spit mud pack instead of a gentle touch or a word? Instead, he obeyed and joyfully accepted healing. God deals with us uniquely. Don't expect Him to deal with you like He does with others. He knows you and knows what you need.

The only reason to look at another's blessing is to rejoice with them in God's provision and goodness and the only reason to look at their sorrow is to encourage, help, and pray for them. When we compare our blessings and trials, we need to listen to the sweet voice of our Saviour, "What is that to thee? Follow thou me."

This question and command will help us put our gaze firmly back on the One who loves us beyond measure. With our focus on Him, we can slip our hand into His and follow Him. He alone can walk the entire length of this valley with us, lead us out of it, and give us peace, joy, and songs in the night.

Psalm 27:8 "*When thou saidst,* Seek ye my face; my heart said unto thee, Thy face, LORD, will I seek."

Chapter Twenty-Seven

God, Our Help

2 Chronicles 16:7b "…Because thou hast relied on the king of Syria, and not relied on the LORD thy God, therefore is the host of the king of Syria escaped out of thine hand."

We looked at Asa, king of Judah, in "Rejoice Alway". His example of praise before the battle encouraged us. We saw he was an excellent king in the beginning. He listened to the man of God and the Word of God, cleansed the land of idols, sacrificed to God, and entered into a covenant with the people of Judah to seek God with their whole heart and soul. He even removed his mother from being queen because she made an idol in a grove. In fact, in chapter 15, God says his heart was perfect.

But then the king of Israel came and laid siege on Judah. Asa immediately took the treasures of the house of God and sent them to the king of Syria, asking for help against Israel. He got the help he needed, and it seemed to turn out well—until the prophet arrived with a message from God.

God rebuked this king with a perfect heart for seeking help from man before asking God for help. Because of this, Asa lost a glorious victory over Syria. Asa got what he asked for, what he wanted, but He missed out on the better thing God had for him.

Asa had forgotten what happened in his first battle when he praised God, asked Him for help, and watched God fight for them. Somewhere along the way, he forgot to praise and seek God in trouble. Instead, he turned to a neighboring king.

Unfortunately, Asa did not repent when he heard God's rebuke. He became angry at Hanani, the prophet, and put him into prison. This marks a downward turn for Asa. Even after Hanani reminded him where he should turn for help, Asa refused. Three years later, when he was sick, Asa turned to doctors, not to God. "...yet in his disease he sought not to the LORD, but to the physicians" (2 Chronicles 16:12).

> Proverbs 3:5-6 "Trust in the LORD with all thine heart; and lean not unto thine own understanding. ^{6}In all thy ways acknowledge him, and he shall direct thy paths."

Asa became another king who started right, but ended wrong. He most likely had Solomon's writings and probably had heard or read the Proverbs of Solomon, including this one. Yet, Asa continued to rely on others, not God, even when God reminded him where he should look.

I have to consider how often I do this. When there is a question, a need, or a concern, do I turn directly to God first? Or do I seek help from others before I ask God? David reminds us that our help comes from the Lord in Psalm 121.

> Psalm 121:1-2 I will lift up mine eyes unto the hills, from whence cometh my help. ^{2}My help cometh from the LORD, which made heaven and earth.

We often ask others as a prayer request. It sounds better that way. "Please pray for me..." Before I ask someone else to pray or help, have I asked God for help? Do I seek God or others first?

> Psalm 61:1-4 "Hear my cry, O God; attend unto my prayer. [2]From the end of the earth will I cry unto thee, when my heart is overwhelmed: lead me to the rock *that* is higher than I. [3]For thou hast been a shelter for me, *and* a strong tower from the enemy. [4]I will abide in thy tabernacle for ever: I will trust in the covert of thy wings. Selah."

Looking at these verses, I see a few things that will help us in times of trouble. In verse 1, we see who we are to cry out to. God is the only One we should turn to in trouble. We are not to cry out against Him and what He has allowed in our lives, but run to Him, and cry out to Him. God is in control and we should always turn to Him. This doesn't mean we never get help from a godly parent, friend, pastor, or counselor. But we should go to God first. He knows which counselor we need.

Verse 2 reminds me there is no place too far away, and no trouble too overwhelming to take to the Rock. Often we try to sort things out on our own, or run to others for help. Yet God is the rock that is higher than I. We are told repeatedly in Scripture that nothing is too hard for God, and He wants us to come to Him and ask when we are in need.

Verse 3 reminds us to look back at God's faithfulness in the past. The Psalmist reminds himself that God has been his shelter and strong tower in the past. Both speak of protection. Remembering God's goodness and protection in the past gives us the confidence to stand firm and make the declaration we see in verse four. "I will abide...I will trust..." He doesn't say he will try to hold on, or trust a little while longer. This is a declaration of intent: "I will." He commits himself to God and vows to trust Him to see him through this trouble.

When I was a single missionary, I remember different trials coming and I would fret and run to God in a panic. What was I going to do? How was He going to fix it this time? I was running to God instead of others, but I wasn't running in faith and confidence. I panicked first, trusted later. When I realized the pattern, it bothered me, so I set out to learn to run to Him in faith, not panic.

I want to be the person who seeks God first, always walking in the confidence that He is in control and He always does right.

Chapter Twenty-Eight

Never Alone

2 Corinthians 1:3-4 "Blessed *be* God, even the Father of our Lord Jesus Christ, the Father of mercies, and the God of all comfort; ⁴Who comforteth us in all our tribulation, that we may be able to comfort them which are in any trouble, by the comfort wherewith we ourselves are comforted of God."

Have you ever been walking through a valley and felt like you were all alone? Oh, you knew you weren't truly alone, and you were thankful for the Lord walking with you. However, when you looked around your circle of friends and acquaintances, you felt like no one else understood, not even those closest to you. Or maybe they had walked your path, but they were out of the valley and on the other side, so you still felt alone.

Then, out of the fog and mist, someone else drew near. Wait! I know them! You mean they're going through this same valley? Somehow, the fog seems less dense. The day seems lighter. You feel better knowing there's someone else walking that same bleak path, like finding a friend to walk with you on a dark night.

A friend and I were talking about this a few years ago. Your heart aches that someone else is experiencing the same pain you are, but you are thankful for the understanding and company. If you both must walk the same path, you're grateful that you can walk together and encourage one another.

I have sometimes asked God why He allowed me to endure the heartache of miscarriages, infertility, and chronic ill health and pain. Then, as I walked along, I came upon a friend walking that same lonely path. She had walked that valley longer than I had. It was a hard path, and she was weary.

I was thankful that I could walk beside her for a while. We shared the valley's heartaches and blessings and encouraged one another to keep our focus on the Lord. We shared the lessons we had learned along the way and drew closer to the Lily of the valleys together. Life was a little sweeter, and our burden a little lighter, by sharing it.

I walked a while longer and found a friend who was new to this valley. Overwhelmed and broken, she struggled to navigate it, wondering why God allowed such suffering. I am thankful I could encourage her as we walked, reminding her of God's goodness, and sharing what I had learned. She was still in the valley, but the path wasn't as lonely or scary when someone else who knew the valley walked with her.

This happened many times through the years. God allowed me to help, encourage, and walk with others who struggled in their valley, just as others walked with me and helped me at my lowest. Not all of them were going through the same thing I endured, but that didn't matter. As we talked and prayed together, I shared the same comfort God gave me in my trials. For a while, I shared their burden, and it encouraged them.

If you're walking through a valley, you'd rather not go through, peer through the mist and see if you can find someone else on your path. It might be you're there to comfort and strengthen them. Possibly, they're here to comfort and strengthen you. Maybe you're both there to draw closer to the Lily of the valleys or to bring Him glory. Whatever God's plan, you're never alone. There is always someone else walking your valley. And that somehow makes it less lonely and easier to bear.

Ecclesiastes 4:9-10 "Two *are* better than one; because they have a good reward for their labour. [10]For if they fall, the one will lift up his fellow: but woe to him *that is* alone when he falleth; for *he hath* not another to help him up."

Sometimes God lets us walk a while without human support or comfort. Maybe we try to reach out, but there isn't much support. Or maybe we're isolated through distance. I've seen many posts over the years, lashing out at others for not being there for them. Resist the temptation to even think like this. God hasn't forsaken you. Resist the temptation to demand support or fall into self-pity because others have someone to help them, but you feel alone. Sometimes God removes or restricts human support and comfort, so we learn to lean on Him alone.

Early in our miscarriages, I began to harbor this discontent. I was on the road, not with family. A few people I talked to had brushed me off, making light of my pain. I wanted Rob to be my comfort, but he didn't seem to know how to help me. Silly of me to expect him to meet my needs, since I didn't even know what I needed, but I built those expectations in my heart and then felt resentful and abandoned when he didn't meet my heart's need.

One night, sitting in a missions apartment, God gently rebuked me for expecting Rob to meet the needs that only God could meet. Was not God my Comforter? Why did I look to my husband for that comfort or long for a friend to comfort and understand? Convicted, I confessed my sin of expecting my help and comfort to come from others.

As I prayed and asked God to comfort my broken heart as only He can, my husband left his chair and sat beside me on the couch. Wrapping his arms around me, he asked, "Having a rough night?" When I looked to God for my comfort, He spoke to my husband's heart, nudging him to comfort me. Rob was not oblivious or callous to my needs. I believe God kept him from seeing how to help me until I turned to God for my comfort. He was trying to teach me (again) that He is all I need.

Never forget that when you feel you're walking alone, the Lily of the valleys is with you. He has promised never to leave us, nor forsake us. Even when we cannot feel or hear Him, He is with us.

> Isaiah 41:10 "Fear thou not; for I *am* with thee: be not dismayed; for I *am* thy God: I will strengthen thee; yea, I will help thee; yea, I will uphold thee with the right hand of my righteousness."

> Isaiah 43:2 "When thou passest through the waters, I *will be* with thee; and through the rivers, they shall not overflow thee: when thou walkest through the fire, thou shalt not be burned; neither shall the flame kindle upon thee."

The enemy wants us to believe that God has forgotten us or forsaken us. He wants us to focus on how others have failed to help. Remember, he is a liar, and the enemy of your soul. As your enemy, he seeks your destruction. Jesus, however, gave His life for you. Which will you choose to believe?

I'd like to leave you with the words to a beautiful and encouraging hymn. May it be your reminder in the middle of your storm that you are never alone. As you draw near the God of all comforts, look around and find someone else in the valley and encourage them.

Never Alone
I've seen the lightning flashing and heard the thunder roll,
I've felt sin's breakers dashing, trying to conquer my soul;
I've heard the voice of my Savior, telling me still to fight on,
He promised never to leave me, never to leave me alone.
No, never alone, no, never alone;
He promised never to leave me, never to leave me alone.*[18]

---

[18] Anonymous, arranged by Baylus B. McKinney. 1895. *Never Alone.* http://library.timelesstruths.org/music/Never_Alone. Public Domain

Chapter Twenty-Nine

Remember or Forget

Psalm 119:52 "I remembered thy judgments of old, O LORD; and have comforted myself."

The Bible has much to say about remembering and forgetting. Unfortunately, we humans often remember and forget the wrong things, especially in times of stress and trials. Studying what God wants us to remember and what He wants us to forget helped me regain focus during one of the long valleys.

Remember our God & His Word

It seems silly to say this. As children of God, we know we are to remember God and His Word, but it is so easy to get busy with our everyday lives or become overwhelmed in our troubles and forget to focus on God. We forget to look for His hand in our circumstances, forget His provision in the past, forget His Word in our busyness, or we read it without focus. We forget Him for minutes, hours, and sometimes days. God reminds us in His Word to *remember Him*!

God's names tell us and remind us of His character (Redeemer, Prince of Peace, God of all Comforts, King of Kings, Father, Jehovah Jireh [our Provider]), etc. Look up the names of God and get a fuller picture of who He is!

> Psalm 63:5-6 "My soul shall be satisfied as *with* marrow and fatness; and my mouth shall praise *thee* with joyful lips: ⁶When I remember thee upon my bed, *and* meditate on thee in the *night* watches."

> Psalm 20:7 "Some *trust* in chariots, and some in horses: but we will remember the name of the LORD our God."

Remember Calvary & the empty grave!

Remembering Calvary can refocus us on God's power and His love. If He can overcome death, nothing I face is too hard for Him. Remembering that He loved me enough to endure Calvary reminds me He still loves me, even when it doesn't feel like it.

> 2 Timothy 2:8 "Remember that Jesus Christ of the seed of David was raised from the dead according to my gospel:"

Remember who He is and meditate on His goodness in the past

Often, the one thing that carries us through our dark days is to remember God's faithfulness in the past. This reminds us He can still deliver us.

> Isaiah 46:9 "Remember the former things of old: for I am God, and there is none else; I am God, and there is none like me,"

> Jonah 2:7 "When my soul fainted within me I remembered the LORD: and my prayer came in unto thee, into thine holy temple."

Remember when David returned to Ziklag and found it burned and his family taken? The men were talking about stoning David. 1 Samuel 30:6 tells us that David encouraged himself in the Lord. We can do the same. Journal some of God's blessings in the past. Then see if you can think of some things to be thankful for in the middle of this trial.

> Psalm 119:55 "I have remembered thy name, O LORD, in the night, and have kept thy law."

> Psalm 78:35 "And they remembered that God *was* their rock, and the high God their redeemer."

> Psalm 103:2 "Bless the LORD, O my soul, and forget not all his benefits:"

Remember God's marvelous works

> 1 Chronicles 16:12 "Remember his marvellous works that he hath done, his wonders, and the judgments of his mouth;"

> Psalm 77:12 "I will meditate also of all thy work, and talk of thy doings."

> Psalm 77:11 "I will remember the works of the LORD: surely I will remember thy wonders of old."

> Psalm 105:5 "Remember his marvellous works that he hath done; his wonders, and the judgments of his mouth;"

> Matthew 16:9 "Do ye not yet understand, neither remember the five loaves of the five thousand, and how many baskets ye took up?"

> Psalm 143:5 "I remember the days of old; I meditate on all thy works; I muse on the work of thy hands."

> Deuteronomy 7:18 "Thou shalt not be afraid of them: *but* shalt well remember what the LORD thy God did unto Pharaoh, and unto all Egypt;"

Remember One Other

> Hebrews 13:3 "Remember them that are in bonds, as bound with them; *and* them which suffer adversity, as being yourselves also in the body."

Colossians 4:18 "The salutation by the hand of me
Paul. Remember my bonds. Grace *be* with you. Amen."

Hebrews 13:7 "Remember them which have the rule
over you, who have spoken unto you the word of God:
whose faith follow, considering the end of *their*
conversation."

Sometimes our trials can help us remember others who need
our prayer. It is easy to focus on ourselves when we suffer. Many
times I have been praying through my pain and God brings to
mind others who need prayer. My suffering has made me more
sensitive to the pain of others. When I pray for them, I forget to
focus on myself. This shift in focus helps restore peace and joy.

Forget the past

Philippians 3:13-15 "Brethren, I count not myself to
have apprehended: but *this* one thing *I do,* forgetting
those things which are behind, and reaching forth unto
those things which are before, [14]I press toward the
mark for the prize of the high calling of God in Christ
Jesus. [15]Let us therefore, as many as be perfect, be thus
minded: and if in any thing ye be otherwise minded,
God shall reveal even this unto you.

Paul chose to forget the past and put it behind him. He could
have focused on his past and all the men and women he had persecuted. Yet, there was no benefit to this, and Paul recognized
that fact. His past was under the blood of Christ. The only thing
it did was spur him on to serve God with the same zeal and passion he used when he persecuted the church of God.

He could have also focused on the past trials and tribula-
tions. When you are in ministry, you will suffer. We expect to
suffer from the world, but somehow we struggle to deal with the
times we suffer from fellow believers or those who name the
name of Christ. Yet, Paul suffered from both and refused to
dwell on it. We only see Paul mention his suffering a few times
in the epistles he wrote. Every time, there was a lesson or

warning attached. He only spoke of these times when it would benefit someone else. He chose to put behind him the things that were past and press toward the mark.

If the past is haunting you, it is time to give it to God and forget it. Every time it comes to mind, remind yourself and the enemy that it is finished and you have given it to God. You refuse to live in the past and let it hold you back from what God wants to do in your life. This is true whether it's your own past sins or someone else's sin against you. Keep your focus on God and what He wants to do with you despite the past. This is the path to peace and victory.

Isaiah 26:3 "Thou wilt keep *him* in perfect peace,
whose mind *is* stayed *on thee:* because he trusteth in thee."

Chapter Thirty

Do the Next Thing

Condensing years of lessons and growth into a few brief chapters carries the risk of sounding like I learned and grew faster than I did. That has the potential to discourage someone. I don't want to do that. My growth came each time I surrendered to something God was teaching me or asking of me. It was simply the result of doing the next thing God put in front of me, learning the next lessons, trusting Him for strength during the next trial.

When we are dropped into the deep end of a valley, everything seems overwhelming. We feel like we're drowning and find it hard to get through the simplest tasks. Give yourself grace as you navigate this trial. Seek the Lord and do the next task in front of you. Don't worry about what's ahead. Leave that in God's capable hands and just do the next thing.

Elisabeth Elliot shared how she was overwhelmed with all there was to do after her husband, Jim, died. The truth of the following poem from an unknown author encouraged her. She went back to the station and simply did the next thing in front of her, not stopping to consider all that needed doing.

Do the Next Thing

From an old English parsonage, down by the sea
There came in the twilight a message to me;
Its quaint Saxon legend, deeply engraven,
Hath, it seems to me, teaching from Heaven.
And on through the doors the quiet words ring
Like a low inspiration: D*o the next thing*.

Many a questioning, many a fear,
Many a doubt, hath its quieting here.
Moment by moment, let down from Heaven,
Time, opportunity, and guidance are given.
Fear not tomorrows, child of the King,
Trust them with Jesus, D*o the next thing.*

Do it immediately, do it with prayer;
Do it reliantly, casting all care;
Do it with reverence, tracing His hand
Who placed it before thee with earnest command.
Stayed on Omnipotence, safe 'neath His wing,
Leave all results, D*o the next thing.*

Looking for Jesus, ever serener,
Working or suffering, be thy demeanor;
In His dear presence, the rest of His calm,
The light of His countenance be thy psalm,
Strong in His faithfulness, praise, and sing.
Then, as He beckons thee, D*o the next thing.*

Maybe you're in a situation with a million tasks to over-whelm. Perhaps you're in a holding pattern, unsure of God's plan for you. Whether the next thing is a daunting task or simply washing your dishes, do it and trust God will guide you on to the next task. Do it, as the poem instructs, immediately, with prayer, relying on Him.

I struggled to get started writing this book. I believed God wanted me to write it. I wanted to share what I had learned to help others, but it was an overwhelming and daunting task. After praying about it and considering it for a while, I shared the burden with my husband. He immediately encouraged me. Then he told someone I was writing a book! That put the pressure on. I was committed.

I still wasn't sure I could do it, so I prayed and did the next thing. I began editing some short blog posts I had written, expanding on them to share what God was teaching me. Each time I got overwhelmed, I asked God what I should do next. He always led. It took a long time to take this from dream to reality. It required simply doing the next thing. Sometimes I had to take breaks from writing because the next thing was trips overseas, extra visa paperwork, teaching opportunities, sickness, counseling, visitors, or dozens of other "interruptions", but God used each of those things to mold me and make this book what it is today.

So, don't get discouraged at obstacles or interruptions, just do the next thing and trust God to lead and work it all out. He orchestrates even the pauses and course changes in our lives.

> Psalm 28:7 "The LORD *is* my strength and my
> shield; my heart trusted in him, and I am helped:
> therefore my heart greatly rejoiceth; and with my song
> will I praise him."

> Psalm 30:11-12 " Thou hast turned for me my
> mourning into dancing: thou hast put off my sackcloth,
> and girded me with gladness; ¹²To the end that *my*
> glory may sing praise to thee, and not be silent. O
> LORD my God, I will give thanks unto thee for ever."

Acknowledgments

This book has my name on it, but I didn't do it alone. I want to thank those who helped the most.

Rob, thank you for nudging me to write, encouraging me, taking care of meals and other chores when I was sick, writing left me exhausted, or when I got engrossed in writing and lost track of time. I appreciate all your input as I asked questions and bounced ideas off you. You listened so patiently and always gave valuable help. Thank you for the writing retreats that gave me desperately needed focused writing time. You are the best husband ever.

Lucia Singleton, thank you for your input and edits. You encouraged me more than you know.

Joshua Lindsey, thank you for proofreading my manuscript. Without your help, this would still be a rough draft.

I also want to thank my family and friends who have encouraged me and urged me on in this journey.

Most of all, I thank God for teaching me, using me, and never giving up on me.

About the Author

Myra Noel Johnson draws on her experiences as a preacher's daughter, single missionary, missionary wife, teacher, and Bible counselor to share the lessons she has learned with others through her writing and speaking. Her greatest desires are to please God and help others. Myra lives in North Dakota with her husband, Rob.

You can find more about Myra and her writing at her website: www.myranoel.com.

www.ingramcontent.com/pod-product-compliance
Lightning Source LLC
Chambersburg PA
CBHW071149120626

46546CB00006B/2180